John Tench

Proposals, Pitches and Beauty Parades

Proposals, Pitches and Beauty Parades

Winning New Business in the '90s

JOHN de FORTE
& GUY JONES

FINANCIAL TIMES

PITMAN PUBLISHING

PITMAN PUBLISHING
128 Long Acre, London WC2E 9AN

A Division of Longman Group UK Limited

First published in Great Britain 1994

British Library Cataloguing in Publication Data
A CIP catalogue record for this book can be obtained from the British Library.

ISBN 0 273 60170 9

Phototypeset in Linotron Times Roman
by Northern Phototypesetting Co. Ltd., Bolton
Printed and bound in Great Britain
by Biddles Ltd, Guildford and King's Lynn

CONTENTS

ACKNOWLEDGEMENTS

Competitive tendering is an emotive topic and people are often reluctant to talk about their own experiences. We are therefore very grateful to the many individuals who have helped us in the preparation and development of this book, including Richard Baker, Maurice Barnfather, Scott Boylan, Andrew Gibb, Julian Griffiths, Peter Hehir, Barry O'Meara, Tim Spratt and John Whitman.

Special thanks are due to Alistair Johnston and his colleagues, with whom many of our ideas have been discussed over a period of several years. Others have also provided information and advice, but have asked not to be mentioned by name.

Again, we express our gratitude to all those who have shared their experiences with us, and emphasise that the views expressed in this book are entirely our own – as are any mistakes or errors of omission.

John de Forte
Guy Jones

London, November 1993

FOREWORD

There are few organisations serving industry today which are not required to compete for work. Tendering has become a permanent feature of the commercial environment, and organisations ignore the skills required to compete effectively at their peril.

We did not choose to call this book *The Proposals Secret*, or by any other title which might suggest that the difference between winning and losing is the application of some magic formula. Experience shows that everything depends on the circumstances and needs of the potential client, and the rigour and imagination with which proposers approach the challenge.

But there are many principles of best practice which hold good for any firm competing through a tender process, regardless of what it is selling. This book attempts to provide a distillation of the principles which underpin successful proposing and to set out a framework within which tenders can be conducted effectively.

WHO THE BOOK WILL HELP

The book focuses on competitive tendering within the business-to-business (and government) context, whether for one-off projects or long-term retained relationships. We have not explicitly dealt with tenders for the provision of physical products – although, as many of the managerial aspects of proposing are the same in the manufacturing sector, the ideas and approaches we have put forward are in some cases equally applicable.

We are principally concerned with proposal situations where firms are competing to convince a potential buyer that they have the most appropriate technical expertise, people, experience, management skills, resources and, of course, charging structure to fulfil a specific set of business needs. This book is therefore relevant not only to the commercial wings of the traditional professions, but also to such diverse industries as construction, advertising, information technology, banking and facilities management.

HOW THE BOOK IS ORGANISED

The structure of the book reflects the most common chronology of a competitive tender – from receiving the invitation to debriefing at the end of the process. This has enabled us to deal with all the key stages which proposers are likely to encounter in the largest, most demanding tenders.

We recognise, of course, that most proposals are on a smaller scale; in some cases, the decision will be taken on the strength of a document or informal meeting alone. Probably the bulk of proposals are undertaken by small teams comprising perhaps only two or three individuals, and do not involve the participation of large numbers across several countries. If we have tended to dwell on the conduct of large proposals, it is only because the logistics of these exercises can be more challenging; and the potential pitfalls increase with the number of people involved. But the principles we espouse apply to tenders of any size.

There are inevitably significant differences in the process between one sector and the next. For example, considerably more importance might be attached to the oral presentation by a food manufacturer seeking to appoint an advertising agency than, say, by a government department wishing to contract out computer services. Once again, we believe that the principles of best practice can be applied with equal force to all industries and types of assignment.

ANECDOTAL MATERIAL

We have deliberately eschewed formal case studies. Given that all proposals are different and that the circumstances and needs of each prospective client are unique, we believe it is unhelpful to cite specific tender experiences as paradigms of best practice.

Moreover, proposing is a confidential activity in which participants on either side do not wish to discuss their successes and failures publicly. We have sought to provide an insight into the attitudes of both clients and suppliers through the use of unattributed quotations drawn from a wide spectrum of industries and organisations.

WHO SHOULD READ THE BOOK

Everyone required to do proposals needs to understand the dynamics of competitive tendering and in each case what the critical success factors are likely to be. Our aim is to answer the team's questions about all aspects of the process and – above all – how to make the most of the opportunity.

For those who have already acquired considerable experience of competitive tendering, we hope the book will prove helpful as a means of refreshing their knowledge and providing a stimulus for further thought. No proposal is ever perfect; and rising client expectations demand that all proposers continue to develop and refine their skills.

Furthermore, to succeed consistently firms must replicate those skills at every level within the organisation; as we stress in the book, clients are increasingly wary of the professional salesman who is brought in to win an assignment, only to disappear afterwards. Some people have a natural flair for proposals and need little formal guidance, but this is no excuse for failing to help others who are less able. Proposal skills should be regarded as a business discipline in their own right, rather than as a set of personal attributes. Everyone who has contact with potential clients will benefit from acquiring a firm grasp of the issues involved.

HOW TO USE THE BOOK

The book performs a dual function. We have set out to provide proposers with a means of acquiring a wider understanding of the commercial context in which tenders arise and, at the same time, to give practical guidance on the conduct of proposals. The book is therefore in part a manual for extracting specific information; readers can refer to the summaries which appear at the end of each chapter to remind themselves of the key issues to be considered as a proposal develops.

It may be helpful, however, to read the book in its entirety before starting work on the next proposal. No aspect of the process should be viewed in isolation and the surest path to success is to get to grips with the process as a whole.

THE LANGUAGE OF PROPOSING

We should briefly mention how we have dealt with the language of proposing. There is a large vocabulary associated with the activity, although many of the expressions in common use are inter-changeable. For example, 'competitive tender', 'proposal', 'pitch' and 'beauty parade' will all be found in the following pages, but each refers in essence to the same activity: formally competing for work.

Individual sectors and industries have their own terminology for describing the process. In the UK, for instance, 'competitive tender' and 'proposal' are the terms preferred by a majority of service providers, including management consultants, accountants, actuaries and construction professionals. Bankers and lawyers often use 'beauty parade'; advertising, public relations and graphic design consultancies tend to talk about 'pitches' and 'new business presentations'. In the US, the term 'competitive tendering' is very rarely used; 'proposals' and 'pitches' are the norm. We have also encountered a number of more metaphorical ways to describe the process, including 'shoot-out' and 'play-off'.

We have not attempted in the book to distinguish between these terms; 'tenders' and 'proposals' are in general our preferred descriptors. In the interests of clarity, however, we consistently use different sets of expressions to describe buyers and sellers. Entities inviting tenders are referred to as 'organisations'; entities on the receiving end are called 'firms'. The meaning of other expressions we have used to describe these two groups is self-evident.

We have also used standard descriptors for the constituent parts of the proposal process. The 'invitation to tender' is the formal means by which a firm is asked to propose, while 'site visits' and 'interviews' are both used to describe the stage at which a firm is given direct access to the potential client in order to prepare its case. The people responsible within a firm for putting the proposal together are defined as 'the proposal team' or 'the team'. 'The proposal' describes the tendering process in its entirety, as opposed to 'the document' or 'the written submission', and 'the oral presentation' or 'the presentation'. Other terms are defined within individual chapters.

1

THE RISE OF THE PROPOSALS PHENOMENON

THE NEW STANDARD

In every corner of the developed world, the market for business services has undergone profound change over the last decade. The effects of these changes have been dramatic, but it is perhaps in the way firms are required to compete for work that the consequences have been most significant.

Competitive tendering is now standard practice across much of industry, and in the public sector too. What forms does it take, and what kind of firms are involved? What are the factors which have impelled buyers to adopt competitive tendering as the principal means of selecting their suppliers, and what do recent trends tell us about the future?

CATEGORIES OF TENDER

Business proposals take many different forms, although all have features in common. In today's marketplace, they can be loosely grouped into four categories:

Regulatory and compliance-driven assignments

It is increasingly common for statutory or de facto compliance needs to be placed out to tender. This encompasses a wide range of functions, from having to present audited accounts under company legislation to the commercial obligation to ensure that employee benefits packages keep pace with changing staff expectations.

The types of firms most usually involved in proposing for assignments of this kind include accountants acting in their capacity as auditors; tax advisers and other specialists; corporate lawyers; insurance brokers acting in their traditional role and also as risk management consultants; stockbrokers in their capacity as portfolio managers; and actuaries as both pensions specialists and employee benefits experts. What unites this otherwise diverse range of services is the requirement for the buyers involved to comply with minimum legislative or commercial standards.

The City beauty parade

While the expression 'beauty parade' is used as a synonym for 'proposal' or 'tender' by most parts of industry, it acquired a more specific connotation in the City during the 1980s. Beauty parades in this sense tend to be concerned with either specific projects or long-term advisory relationships where the potential client does not necessarily have a particular requirement in mind.

Thus an accounting firm might be asked to propose for the task of acting as reporting accountants in a flotation or in raising capital on the equity markets; stockbrokers may have to compete for the job of sponsor; lawyers for the role of legal adviser; financial PR consultants as promoter; and, of course, merchant bankers as financial advisers and underwriters to the issue. The same groups of professionals might also be asked to undergo a beauty parade where an organisation is seeking to appoint – or replace – advisers to whom it can turn for general advice or when a specific project arises at a future date. Because of the need to comply with Stock Exchange rules, assignments of this nature have a strong regulatory dimension; but they are equally concerned with the marketing of companies to the investment community.

Development projects

Development projects essentially comprise any form of work or advice related to physical infrastructure – in most cases, this will involve construction and property. They also encompass assignments associated with changes in management systems, corporate structure or even culture.

On the construction and property side, there is a wide range of advisers and specialists who will be asked to tender. This includes civil engineers, surveyors, architects and quantity surveyors, as well as other professionals such as interior designers and space planners. Commercial developers, of course, might be asked to tender for the redevelopment of a particular site or area, while management consultants will commonly be invited to propose as project managers.

Management consultants will be even more heavily involved in tenders for specific corporate development projects. They, and a miscellany of other business service providers, compete every day for the opportunity to advise on the selection and implementation of computer hardware and software, telecommunications strategy, management change programmes and a host of other projects concerned with improving an organisation's overall efficiency and, therefore, competitiveness.

Creative pitches

There are tenders where the preparation and presentation of original concepts is usually the focus of attention. Firms whose proposals fall into this category include advertising agencies, PR consultancies and graphic designers. They are joined by a vast array of other marketing services companies, such as direct mail, sales promotion and sponsorship specialists.

Inevitably, there is considerable overlap between each of the above four categories: Big Six firms of international accountants, for example, compete in at least the first three. Moreover, nearly all the firms mentioned above will also be tendering for services and advice from each other.

THE COMMERCIAL CONTEXT

Tendering has a long history. Creative service providers, such as advertising agencies and PR consultancies, have always acquired the majority of their new and, indeed, repeat business through pitches against other agencies. Design consultants, architects and management consultants have also traditionally won new contracts in the same way – very few projects are likely to be awarded to these firms without their having taken part in some kind of formal competition.

On the other hand, the same clients have been comparatively slow to exercise a similar discipline in choosing professional advisers, whether lawyers, accountants or bankers. For a long time, assignments were simply handed to the firms which buyers knew and trusted most; quite often, these relationships existed (and were renewed year after year) primarily for historical reasons. One can still find law firms working for companies which they have advised for half a century or more, and where the sons and grandsons of owner–managers continue to instruct the same firm that their fathers and grandfathers relied on when the business was founded. We can be certain, however, that the number of such long-established relationships is considerably smaller now that it was 20 years ago. This has been brought about by a combination of factors.

Increased client expectations

In Britain, the Thatcher revolution has had a profound effect on many areas of business practice. During the late 1970s and early 1980s, the buyers of business and advisory services began to want more from the firms which provided them; gradually, the balance of power began to shift from service providers to buyers. Companies and institutions realised they there was no reason why they had to endure indifferent or poor service, slow response times, arcane or incomprehensible advice, and only limited accountability with regard to fees. What was to stop a chief executive approaching another group of advisers if he felt the incumbents were failing to meet his company's needs? His predecessor may have used the firm for the last 15 years, but that was no longer an adequate reason automatically to follow the same path.

The business world was becoming more complex, more international and, indeed, more frightening. If a company wished to prosper in a tougher commercial environment, it needed the active support of professionals who were able to contribute real value in the performance of their role and, preferably, on a wider canvas as well. Things needed to happen faster, professionals were expected to acquire a better grasp of the industry sectors in which their clients were doing business, and everyone needed to keep a tighter rein on costs.

Specialisation was also becoming more important. From employment law to anti-trust and competition statutes, a raft of new legislation made the generalist adviser an increasingly risky option. Clients needed the reassurance and comfort that could only come from hiring professionals with highly specialist knowledge.

Closer scrutiny of costs, the growing need for advisers who could contribute genuine value, and the requirement for a greater depth of industry and technical expertise did not immediately lead to widespread competitive tendering. Nevertheless, the confluence of these trends certainly helped to erode traditional loyalties and to reinforce the view that it made commercial sense to adopt more stringent approaches to their appointment.

Changing attitudes towards the value of business services

The corollary of this was a closer examination of the value of the tasks which buyers needed their service providers to perform, especially where that task was statutorily imposed. Particularly from the mid-1980s, both corporate and private buyers came increasingly to regard compliance-related professional services as little more than commodities to be purchased at the lowest possible price.

This heralded the beginning of a new wave of both private and corporate consumerism. For example, residential conveyancing and company audits were viewed more consciously as formalities which brought little benefit to the buyer obliged to pay for them. Both a conveyance and an audit may require expertise and experience, but growing numbers of individuals and companies took advantage of a more competitive climate to insist on lower prices. After all, they argued, one audit or conveyance is very like another, and – since all that matters is whether the function is performed – there was no advantage to be gained from paying more than was strictly necessary to meet a purely legal obligation.

Thus formal tenders began to be issued by the larger companies, estimates of professional fees were sought in advance of a given assignment and, particularly in the legal sector, private clients shopped around for the lowest price before deciding which firm to instruct. To their delight, buyers discovered that, when challenged on cost, many professional advisers were surprisingly willing to lower their fees – sometimes to absurdly low levels – if the choice was between some work or none at all, especially when the market began to turn down at the end of the 1980s.

Deregulation

The 1980s were characterised by an unprecedented deregulation of markets and abolition of restrictive practices. From the City's 'Big Bang' to the ending of the utilities monopolies, the application of free-market principles to a previously moribund British economic infrastructure created new and lucrative areas of work for professional advisers. At the same time, however, deregulation required firms to acquire still further specialist knowledge and to fight more aggressively for assignments against larger numbers of competitors.

During the same period, the professions themselves were deregulated to a considerable extent. The mid- and late 1980s saw professional bodies throughout the construction, accounting and legal sectors weaken or abolish the restrictions on marketing, recruitment, capital structure and in a variety of other areas. Inter alia, the newly bestowed freedom to organise and promote themselves in a manner more like that of their corporate clients gave rise to larger firms with deeper pockets, a wider range of specialists and a less passive approach to the development of new business. The net result was yet more and tougher competition for work.

Quality issues

The American philosophy of Total Quality Management found its way across the Atlantic in the mid-1980s. As with so many US business practices, it took firm root among large numbers of European and especially British companies. Combined with more traditional quality programmes such as BS 5750, the net effect has been to move quality issues to the top of the management agenda.

Companies no longer look only to the suppliers of physical goods to meet minimum performance criteria; precisely the same is now expected of their professional advisers. That in turn means a tighter focus on quality, a greater willingness to change when standards slip and the determination to put firms through their paces by making them compete for work.

Economic recession

On both sides of the Atlantic, the seemingly endless post-war boom finally ground to a halt with the 1973 energy crisis. The remainder of the decade was characterised by high inflation, low or negative growth, industrial unrest and practically every other symptom of economic decline, and it was not until well into the first half of the 1980s that conditions finally improved. Even then, the period of rapid expansion which followed had quickly burned itself out by the beginning of the current decade and, in so doing, plunged the developed world into a recession which, unlike that of the early 1980s, has had a particularly damaging effect on the service sector.

Depressed conditions make every organisation examine the value it derives from its suppliers. More significantly, however, the latest recession has prompted large numbers of commercial and public sector organisations to look for root and branch ways of reducing fixed overheads. The answer for many has been to contract out in-house services, ranging from catering and graphic design to credit control and data processing. The trend towards contracting out creates significant opportunities for professional advisers, but – because the process is predicated on competitive tendering – these will be seized only by firms able to master the disciplines involved.

Furthermore, the days are over when professional advisers could rely exclusively on their personal contacts for work, were unchallenged on fees, could leave service issues to chance, and needed to do only what they were asked and no more. The principles which underpin successful competitive tendering are precisely those which will determine the long-term prosperity of firms doing business in the commercial environment of the 1990s.

SECTOR TRENDS

What effects have intensifying competition, heightened client expectations, greater cost-consciousness and deregulation had on the business services sector? A brief survey of the professions in Britain serves to illustrate the consequences.

Accountancy

A survey of major UK companies conducted in 1992 revealed that one-fifth of all audits are now put out to tender as a matter of corporate policy. A number of factors lie behind this development.

In 1984, the accounting profession was permitted by its governing body to advertise for the first time. After a largely unproductive and costly flirtation, the larger firms began to look to other elements in the marketing mix and, over time, to recruit in-house specialists in everything from media relations and direct mail to conference organisation and graphic design. The volume and diversity of marketing activity increased dramatically, helping to stimulate already growing levels of competition.

Probably the single most critical factor in the acceleration of competitive tendering was merger activity among the then Big Eight and other large firms during the second half of the 1980s. With the creation of significantly larger national and international partnerships, many clients found themselves with new auditors and advisers in whose selection they had not participated; there were often clear conflicts of interest within the enlarged client base. The response – some accountants might call it revenge – of many companies to this imposition was go out to tender, making the incumbent firm justify and fight for the business in competition with its rivals.

There are two tendering landmarks for British accountants. In 1986, Britain's largest company, ICI, placed its audit out to competitive tender – the most significant such competition ever seen by the profession. The winning firm set new standards for the professionalism of its proposal, which for several years afterwards was regarded by many as the paradigm of best proposal practice.

In 1990, Britain's largest insurer, Prudential Corporation, undertook a similar exercise. The British economy was heading for recession and the cost of audit services had by this stage become a critical issue. Prudential was also looking for concrete signs from the firms involved that their audit would do more than simply meet statutory requirements in exchange for a competitive price; it would make a wider contribution to management decision-making through a more business-orientated approach to risk. However, this issue was obscured when the winning firm's proposal docu-ment was leaked to the press – the document showed how far some firms were willing to discount their fees in order to secure pre-stigious appointments.

The Prudential tender was important for the UK profession

because the decision-making criteria illustrated how the attitudes of large corporate buyers had changed. Not only were companies expecting greater competitiveness and accountability on fees; they needed to be convinced that the audit would provide an additional management tool as well as simply meeting a legal requirement. Thus accountants had to find a way of redirecting the focus of audit away from straightforward 'tick and bash' towards a more thorough assessment of internal management controls and wider business risk.

This has a number of far-reaching consequences. A more judgmental approach to the audit has meant that partner and manager time as a proportion of total audit hours is on the increase, at the expense of junior resources (thus further squeezing margins); and industry specialists, not necessarily with an accountancy background, are being drafted onto audit teams in increasing numbers. However, the demand for a higher value audit does give firms the opportunity to differentiate themselves by demonstrating a better understanding of the client's business, and the expertise and experience needed to make often highly subjective assessments. In the longer term, this will help firms to defend their margins and resist further pressure to reduce their prices.

Legal services

Tendering has not affected British corporate lawyers to anything like the same extent as accountants, although the picture is changing rapidly.

In 1984 and again in 1987, the Law Society relaxed the restrictions governing advertising and promotion by the profession, resulting in an explosion of marketing activity among law firms. Two years later, legislation was introduced which sought to end the solicitors' monopoly on residential conveyancing, thus threatening to disintegrate the bedrock upon which the bulk of British lawyers' fee income is based. Although in practice very few new competitors have subsequently entered the field, the prospect of greater competition combined with a more consumerist approach on the part of clients resulted in heavy discounting which remains to this day.

At the same time, British companies beginning to place audit and other financial advisory services out to tender as a matter of course began to ask their lawyers to undergo the same process. The beauty parade had arrived.

In early 1993, the British-based multinational Allied Lyons set out to rationalise the 100-plus law firms it was using throughout the UK. An invitation to tender was issued to the major incumbents; these were asked to submit a formal written response, after which a smaller number of practices were selected to make an oral presentation. The Allied Lyons tender quickly became something of a *cause célèbre* within the British legal profession; its scale was unprecedented, and the approach taken came as an unwelcome surprise to the majority of firms which took part.

A competition of this nature would have been a routine experience for a Big Six firm of accountants but, to many British lawyers, the tender epitomised everything that was unnerving about the new environment. A corporation with which many firms had worked for years was suddenly asking them to specify charge-out rates, describe how they would manage the fee relationship, identify specific individuals to undertake particular kinds of work, and discuss how their resources and experience would be brought to bear in delivering genuine benefits for the company. None was an unreasonable request, but each caused widespread confusion, consternation and, in many cases, resentment.

The Allied Lyons tender was not the first of its kind and will by no means be the last. But it illustrated clearly enough that many law firms have yet to invest in the development of proposal skills and are still unfamiliar with the disciplines involved.

Advertising and marketing

Although advertising, PR and design agencies have always had to compete for new business, it is only in recent years that clients have begun to subject them to rigorous scrutiny. Increasingly, marketing services companies are being required by their clients to repitch on an annual basis and, in many cases, to submit formal proposals against their competitors for individual projects.

Greater pressure is being put on agencies to demonstrate their ability to monitor and control costs; it is no longer safe to rely on the creative dimension alone to win on assignment. Proposers must show that they understand the objectives and commercial context of the account, and have effective systems for measuring progress. The trend from commission- to fee-based remuneration is also encouraging agencies to be more objective about which types of marketing activity they recommend. There is a far greater focus on research, planning and project management skills; the days when less business-like agencies could secure a new account through bright ideas alone are fast receding. It is likely that the proposal disciplines which are already of critical importance to other professions will play a growing role in helping agencies to win new business.

Other advisers

The requirement for prospective advisers to participate in tenders has spread throughout the commercial world. The larger insurance brokers, for example, began to be asked by their potential clients to submit proposals some 15 years ago but, as with audit services, corporate buyers are placing more and more emphasis on added value, service delivery and quality.

Tendering has always been an integral feature of the construction industry but, as in so many other fields, the traditional concentration on price has widened to encompass a broader range of issues. In addition, firms which advise the construction and property sector are increasingly obliged to submit formal proposals on a project-by-project basis; civil engineers, surveyors, property and project managers are among those affected.

The same is true in banking, stockbroking and other financial advisory services. Where once a firm would have secured appointment on the strength of its reputation and network of personal relationships, potential buyers now expect written submissions and formal presentations. While time constraints militate against the use of formal proposals for urgent rights issues or tactical acquisitions, it is now commonplace for large companies to select their brokers, clearing and investment bankers through this means.

THE PUBLIC SECTOR

Perhaps the area where tendering has grown most rapidly in recent years has been in the public sector; for a number of reasons, it is set to increase. While the following comments relate to developments in the UK, the underlying trends are equally pronounced in other parts of the developed world.

Privatisation

Selling off large parts of the state-owned sector has helped to engender a climate in which competition, efficiency and value for money become key imperatives for those institutions and agencies left in public hands.

Over the last ten years, many of the bastions of Britain's nationalised industries have been transferred to private ownership: telecommunications, steel production, the national airline, and the electricity and water utilities to name only a few. It is only a small step from the disposal of state assets to the application of free-market principles to local and national government services. The Government has had little hesitation in taking that step.

Contracting-out

Local government witnessed the first experiments. During the mid-1980s, Conservative-controlled councils up and down the country began contracting out services such as refuse collection and street cleaning. The trend quickly spread to a wide variety of other services, from building maintenance and housing management to data processing and catering.

Compulsory Competitive Tendering

The commercial imperative which underpinned the contracting-out of services was given a new and powerful stimulus by the 1988 Local Government Act. This introduced the concept of Compulsory Competitive Tendering – CCT – which, as the name suggests, requires in-house departments of local councils and boroughs to demonstrate that they can win work against private sector service suppliers. Not only are the so-called 'blue collar' services such as waste disposal to be placed out to tender, but also those of a professional nature, such as legal and computing services. The legislation provides for this extension of CCT to be implemented from 1995 onwards, but several local authorities have already begun the process voluntarily.

CCT is opening up major opportunities for professional service providers of all kinds. As we write, the criteria which will govern the selection process is still under discussion. The legislative framework as currently proposed will not oblige local authorities to accept the lowest-priced tender; they will instead have the flexibility to adopt a wider (and as yet undecided) variety of measures including, for example, service quality. In some areas, the Government has rejected the so-called 'double-envelope' system, whereby competing firms must first meet a minimum quality threshold, after which the final decision would have to be taken solely on the basis of price.

This decidedly invidious approach was terminally discredited by the tendering of independent television franchises in 1992. The system enabled some existing franchisees to retain enormously lucrative franchises on nominal bids of £1,000 a year because they were certain they had no competitors, while others lost to bidders of unproven quality who were prepared to pay astronomically inflated licence fees. The rejection of the double-envelope system shows that firms competing for work under the CCT regime will have to do more than just beat the in-house team on price; as in the private sector, they will need to demonstrate quality, efficiency and other benefits.

Market testing

Launched in November 1992, 'market testing' is the central government equivalent of CCT. One year later, approximately £1.5 billion of government activity such as IT, payroll and library services had been put out to tender, encompassing the activities of nearly 45,000 civil servants. Considerably larger tranches are to be exposed to market testing before 1997 which, amounting to some £20 billion, represent roughly half the annual running costs of the UK civil service.

The programme is still in its infancy, and there is considerable confusion within both the public and private sectors about tendering procedure, selection criteria and the fairness with which the bids of in-house departments are assessed against those of external competitors. For example, comparisons of pricing structures present major difficulties: so many of the costs of an in-house government department are defrayed across the entire government bureaucracy, and can be impossible to compare accurately because Whitehall does not use commercially accepted accounting standards. Moreover, many potential bidders in the private sector are sceptical about their chances of success against internal departments unless the project involves the injection of new skills or a physical 'output' of some kind, such as reports. Where a private sector organisation is being invited to bid for precisely the same service as that currently provided by the in-house team, there is a suspicion that the pricing issue will scupper their proposal every time.

The problems inherent in comparing external with internal tenders remain to be resolved but, whatever the imperfections of the process, few service providers can afford to ignore the opportunities being created by market testing.

'Charterism'

While instituting tender programmes to secure greater value for money, the Government has at the same time been seeking to instil higher standards of services and quality in public service organisations through the medium of a Citizen's Charter. Created for institutions such as the National Health Service and Inland Revenue, individual charters lay down a minimum series of performance standards which users can reasonably expect from public bodies; where they fail, the charter sets out procedures for redress which, in some cases, involve financial compensation. Dismissed by many as a public relations exercise which provides little tangible benefit to the general public, the Citizen's Charter is nevertheless encouraging more competitive practices throughout both the public and private sectors.

The European Community

Putting public sector services out to tender is not, of course, the sole prerogative of the British Government; the European Community, for example, is itself a significant buyer of external services. The European Commission, in contrast to UK national and local government, has in many cases established clear rules for the evaluation of service providers' proposals which may provide a blueprint for the member states themselves to follow.

A contract is unlikely to be awarded on the basis of price alone. For instance, in the points system used by the EC to select firms of lawyers, 30 per cent are allocated to assessment of cost; 40 per cent relate to technical expertise; 20 per cent to the proposed approach to and management of the assignment; and the remaining 10 per cent to track record and experience.

On a wider front, the EC has also been seeking to address the basis on which public procurement should be organised by member governments. In 1987, the Commission announced a reform package designed to open up the procurement of public services to larger numbers of firms, and to make tendering and award procedures more transparent. The objective was to increase intra-Community competition and put an end to governments awarding contracts without publishing their reasons for doing so.

Progress on implementing the subsequent directives has been painfully slow. But the Commission's interest in the issues involved provides further confirmation that public sector tendering within the EC will continue to assume greater significance – not least because, in time, a more level playing field throughout the Community is likely to be mandated by Brussels.

A BRAVE NEW WORLD . . .

For any service provider who ever doubted it, there is clearly no shortage of evidence to demonstrate that the brave new world of competitive tendering affects practically every area of commercial and public sector activity. Indeed, it is no exaggeration to claim that nearly all functions of any size or significance requiring external involvement are now put out to tender. Firms which earn their living by selling expertise and experience must therefore acquire highly developed proposal skills if they are to succeed in an increasingly competitive environment.

2

RESPONDING TO THE INVITATION

FORM AND CONTEXT OF THE INVITATION

The proposal process usually begins with the arrival of a formal invitation to tender. From that moment onwards, you are involved in an endeavour which is not dissimilar to a military campaign: victory will depend on your ability to marshall resources effectively; to read the minds of your adversaries, and know their strengths and weaknesses; and to turn *your* strengths to decisive advantage. It will also depend on timing, luck, and above all, meticulous planning.

The most important point, however, is that this campaign starts the moment you receive the invitation – not when you submit your proposal document, or turn up at the presentation. There is a natural tendency for proposers to be casual about the early stages of a tender, and then to work up to a frenzy as the deadline for the document or presentation approaches. This is a mistake. All stages of the proposal process are transparent to the potential client, who will be observing you – and assessing you – from the moment you receive the invitation.

Our experience suggests that possibly one-third of all proposals are effectively decided before the competing firms have made a formal submission: not because the clients know from the beginning which supplier they are going to choose, but because the contenders have already made a strong impression – good or bad – during the early phases of the process.

Before you rush into battle, however, you need to consider the form of the invitation and the context in which it has been issued. Both need to be taken into account in deciding how to respond.

Invitations to tender take many forms, but among the most common are:

- a written brief
- an interview
- request for credentials
- public advertisement
- a combination of the above.

A written brief

This is the most orthodox form of invitation. The written brief could be just a letter, outlining in broad terms what is required of the prospective service provider, and indicating the procedure by which the successful firm is to be selected; or, at the other end of the spectrum, it could be a detailed questionnaire supplied with copious information on the organisation which is conducting the tender. A thorough written brief usually suggests that the organisation is in earnest about putting the service out to tender, and not merely 'window shopping'.

An interview

In this case the tendering organisation requests an interview with one or more prospective suppliers in order to explain the nature of the task and the organisation's requirements. Such a meeting should be carefully prepared for; however casual the interviewee may appear, this is a golden opportunity to extract critical information and to begin to convey the right messages. Any meeting with the prospective client in the early stages of the proposal is of crucial importance. The topic is covered in detail in Chapter 6.

Request for credentials

'Credentials' in this context refer to all material which will substantiate your firm's qualifications to provide particular services: track record, client list, examples of relevant projects conducted in the past, staff numbers, management structure and so on. They comprise, in effect, your firm's CV. Credentials may be required in the form of a document or oral presentation.

A request for credentials does not necessarily presage the beginning of a proposal process, although it is often the means by which an organisation which is contemplating putting a service out to tender draws up a shortlist of contenders. Although it is unusual in this situation to be given much information about the organisation or its requirements, it pays to show that you have done your homework and have some understanding of its image in the marketplace and the objectives of the management team. When you are asked for credentials, therefore, do not merely send a brochure on your firm. Try to tailor your response to what you know about the organisation, even if this amounts to no more than a passing reference. Also, you can convey more about how your firm operates through case studies than through a dry narrative on its attributes: so it is generally right to include some.

Public advertisement

This practice is particularly common in the public sector. It is not an invitation in the usual sense, as the tendering organisation is using a mass medium to attract enquiries from potential bidders. Generally a written brief will be sent to firms which respond to the advertisement.

While the form of the invitation gives some indication of the tendering organisation's intentions, the context in which it is issued can provide a useful early insight into your prospects for success. By 'context' we principally mean whether your firm has an existing relationship with the organisation, and whether you knew in advance that the service was about to be put out to tender. The circumstances in which you could be invited to participate in a proposal process are obviously varied, but for the purposes of this discussion we are concerned with five basic categories:

(i)   the invitation is the culmination of a deliberate targeting campaign;
(ii)   you have some form of existing working relationship – acting, possibly, for the organisation in another capacity;
(iii) you have only informal contacts with the organisation;
(iv)   there is no existing relationship;
(v)   you are the incumbent for the service being offered for proposal.

As in any competitive activity, it is always possible to win a proposal by 'coming from behind'; but it is as well to know beforehand what your handicap is. In this respect, points (i) to (iv) above represent a sliding scale of opportunity.

If the invitation is a logical step towards getting closer to the organisation, and you have taken trouble, over a period of time, to find out its objectives and to court its decision-makers, then clearly you start with an advantage. If you have a working relationship in some other capacity, you should in normal circumstances be able to put forward a cogent case for extending the relationship (although professional advisers, like actors, often suffer from type-casting). Even purely informal contacts, although usually inferior to the above, can be leveraged to good effect. For example, you may be able to elicit some information from your contacts on why the service is being put out to proposal and what the prevailing political climate is within the organisation. But without any relationship at all, you may ask yourself: if we don't have an inside track, who does? This isn't to suggest that winning is beyond your grasp; only that you might be further back on the starting grid than some of the other contenders.

Where you are the incumbent, the invitation must be seen in a rather different light. The obvious question is: if the client is happy with the service he is receiving from you, why go out to tender? The reasons may not be sinister – in some areas, such as the public sector, periodic reviews of suppliers is *de rigueur* – or going to the trouble of a proposal process may just be an attempt to persuade you to reduce your fees. Often, however, you may feel that the inside track afforded by being the incumbent will actually turn out to be the end of the road. Retaining business through a proposal calls for many of the same tactics you would use in attempting to win new business, although the need for an honest appraisal of where you stand at the beginning of the process is even more imperative; this is a subject to which we will return later.

Another factor you should take into account in assessing your ultimate chances of success is whether or not you have been given prior warning about the tender. This is the sort of inside track that can put you firmly on the path to victory. Advanced notice will give you extra time to undertake some preparatory research on the company; consider how you are going to approach the proposal process; select the team according to your preferred criteria (rather than, as often happens, having to choose on the basis of availability, not capability); and find out more from the company itself about the motivations for and objectives of the tender. At the other end of the spectrum, the incumbent firm which has no inkling that a proposal is about to take place until the invitation arrives in the post must be said to start with a distinct disadvantage.

Participating in a competitive tender consumes vast quantities of firms' most precious commodity, time. It is sensible, therefore, to try to assess at the outset what the probability is that a particular invitation directed to your firm will eventually lead to actual revenue. You need to take into account both your competitive position at the beginning of the proposal process and whether you believe the target organisation is seriously committed to employing external advisers in the near future. Sometimes the circumstances will enable you to make an accurate judgement; but, in the absence of more precise information, the form and context of the invitation can give a helpful indication of where you stand. It may even be worth considering these two factors together, as in the matrix below:

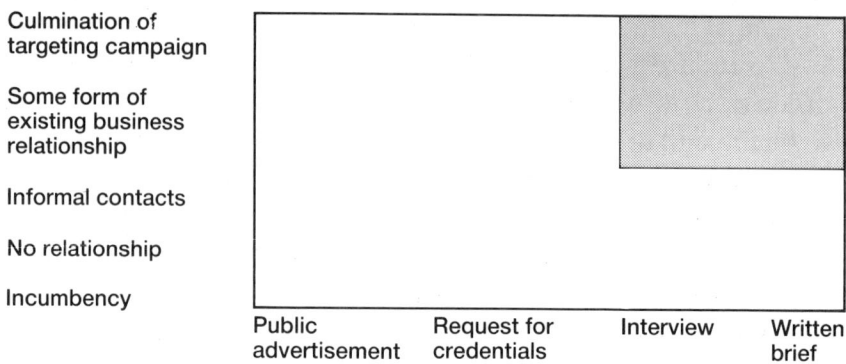

Culmination of
targeting campaign

Some form of
existing business
relationship

Informal contacts

No relationship

Incumbency

Public   Request for   Interview   Written
advertisement   credentials   brief

Figure 2.1   Circumstances of the invitation

The circumstances are likely to be most propitious where both
the form and context of the invitation are favourable – as indicated
by the top right hand corner of the matrix. This method can hardly
be described as having the properties of a crystal ball, but at least it
might provide a basis on which to gauge how extensive your
investment in the proposal should be; or, if you have a number of
proposals running at the same time, which should be accorded the
greatest priority.

SHOULD WE DECLINE THE INVITATION?

In making this assessment of the invitation, and of your ultimate
chances of success, you need to ask a more fundamental question:
should we accept the invitation at all? There are a number of
circumstances where you might have reason to think twice:

- you suspect that the 'playing field is uneven' and you have no
  genuine chance of success
- you doubt the seriousness of the organisation's intentions
- the costs of proposing may outweigh the financial benefits of
  winning the work
- the assignment itself may not be profitable

- the assignment may expose your firm to unacceptable business risks
- existing commitments mean you are unable adequately to resource the assignment – or the proposal itself
- your firm does not have the relevant expertise, or for some other reason you are unable to present a credible proposal
- your firm is the incumbent.

The uneven playing field

This is a most difficult area, for you will often have to make a decision based on little more than intuition. There are two main reasons why you may find yourself being asked to compete on unequal terms: possibly the organisation has no intention of changing suppliers, but hopes to use the proposal process to pressure its incumbents into reducing costs; or it has already effectively decided to employ a firm other than your own, but feels the need to rationalise and justify its decision by going through the motions of a tender.

If you suspect that either of these might apply, some tactful questioning of the target organisation early on in the process may help to clarify the position. You may get an evasive answer, but it should provide some indication of whether or not you are about to enter a fair contest. With a suitably diplomatic line of questioning, you should be able to establish the motivations for putting the service out to tender without giving the impression that you think the whole process is a foregone conclusion.

In practice, few organisations set up and run a tendering process knowing the outcome at the beginning. The proposal process is time-consuming and disruptive for the prospective client as well as for the competing firms; most will not waste their time – or yours.

Are they serious?

This is a more common problem, one that tends to afflict sectors such as advertising, PR and design rather more than the traditional professions. The risk is that the organisation is looking for ideas and is not necessarily intending to pay for them. Tell-tale signs that the organisation may not be entirely serious about employing external advisers include: the absence of a formal brief; vagueness about the process by which the advisers will be selected; reluctance to hold a meeting to discuss the proposal; and a lack of candour about the budgets available for the assignment.

The chief executive of one financial PR company describes how he scrutinises approaches which may be of dubious value in the following terms:

> I'm very cautious about invitations that come out of the blue through the post – it usually means big pitch lists or half-hearted fishing around. So I 'phone up whoever it is and talk to them, and then I can decide whether it's worth pursuing – whether they've got the money, how many other firms they've asked, whether they can supply a proper brief (if they can't, it's a bad sign) – basically, whether they sound as though they are serious. Pitching takes a lot of time and money, and I'll certainly say no if I don't think it's going to lead anywhere. No-one likes to turn down an invitation in this business, but you've got to try to cut out the timewasters.

Being observant is a critical skill in winning proposals, but it is of equal value in deciding whether it is appropriate to accept the invitation.

It is not only in the private sector that hard questions need to be asked about whether an invitation is genuine. As we suggested in the previous chapter, the current vogue for market testing in the public sector must also be treated with a degree of scepticism. Often the objective of the exercise is to establish how competitive in cost terms in-house departments are in comparison with external contractors, and to pick up some hints along the way on how to create efficiencies and operational improvements. It does not necessarily lead to projects being sourced externally, although by the time the contractor realises this he may have already invested much time and effort.

The costs and benefits of proposing

If you believe that the proposal process is likely to represent an investment which exceeds the financial benefit of winning the work, there can be no harm in suggesting to the prospective client that a less onerous means of selecting the winning firm would be more appropriate. You may even be asked to help develop an alternative approach, which can only promote your chances of success.

The financial benefit, incidentally, may not always be easy to define. You will need to take into account whether the assignment is recurring, like an annual audit, or a one-off project; and whether, if the latter, it is likely to lead to follow-up work. You also need to assess the opportunities for cross-selling other services into the organisation, especially where these might represent a larger fee or a bigger profit margin than the service for which you have been asked to tender.

Ultimately, though, if you do not believe it is commercially sound to participate in a proposal it is better to say so and withdraw, than to accept the invitation and put in insufficient effort. That can only create a poor impression, one which will probably disqualify you from participating in future tenders conducted by that organisation. Your performance during the proposal process is likely to be remembered long after the tender itself is over.

Profitability of the assignment

You may have no idea how profitable an assignment is likely to be at the beginning of a proposal, not least because agreement on fee usually occurs only in the later stages. Firms are often expected to do the job for low or sometimes no profit, just for the privilege of establishing a relationship with a prestigious client. Deciding to participate in such circumstances must therefore be a matter of commercial judgement. If you suspect that an assignment is unlikely to yield an acceptable level of profit, it is best to discuss this with the target organisation at an early stage. Otherwise you are wasting everyone's time.

Unacceptable business risks

These may occur, for example, when an organisation is planning to outsource a service to a contractor in order to reduce costs, but is hoping at the same time to impose an unlimited liability clause in the event of the contractor's under-performance or non-performance of the assignment. In such circumstances, the professional indemnity costs for the contractor might not be built into the fees, and could therefore represent an unacceptable risk. As such issues are usually resolved at the negotiation stage following the proposal process, it may be premature to decline an invitation on these grounds. Where possible, it is best to discuss the issue early and to express a view during the proposal, without at that stage committing your firm to a contractual obligation.

Another type of business risk may arise from being associated with an organisation of dubious reputation. This must be a matter of judgement for the proposal leader.

Finally, you need to consider whether winning the work may jeopardise a relationship with an existing client, through perceived conflicts of interest. It is common sense that any issues relating to potential conflicts should be discussed with both the existing client and potential client before accepting the invitation to tender.

Unavailability of resources

Not having the appropriate resources available is one of the best reasons for declining an invitation to tender; to pretend that you can staff an assignment when you can't will cost you much more in the long run than foregoing the opportunity to pitch for a new piece of business. Indeed, complete honesty can pay unexpected dividends; one chairman of a communications consultancy quotes a vivid example from personal experience:

> A company we had been courting for five years asked us to pitch. Because of two recent large wins, we couldn't do the work at that time, but I told him that we would be in a position to do it four months later. He was so impressed by this, he left it until we were ready and simply

gave us the business without a pitch. It wasn't a tactic; had we taken him on and failed, we would have blown a major long term opportunity.

This may be a rather exceptional case. But the most important point is that successful professional relationships must be built on trust. To deceive a potential client during the proposal process will wreck that relationship forever.

Lack of credibility

In most circumstances, you are unlikely to find yourself on a shortlist unless your firm has the skills and expertise to meet the requirements of the assignment. There may be circumstances where you have most of the skills required to do the job, but there is a gap in a specific area – in this case, you might consider a joint proposal with an organisation which has complementary expertise or drafting an outside specialist onto your team. But if you are asked to tender for a project which you are manifestly ill-equipped to perform, no useful purpose can be served by accepting the invitation. As with other forms of business-to-business and professional services marketing, success in proposals will come from a highly targeted approach, not by trying to win work from anyone in a position to provide it. In the public sector, where tenders are often advertised, it is not unusual for a plethora of firms to apply for the tendering documentation, although very few will be qualified to do the work. According to the divisional director of one of the UK's largest suppliers of computer services to the public sector:

> After the tender is advertised, they might get 50 or 60 responses. On the bigger contracts, though, only eight or so respondents will be credible, and only three or four will be serious contenders.

The clear message is: conserve your energy and resources for the tenders you can win; do not be seduced into dissipating your resources on proposals where your prospects are remote.

Incumbency

Attitudes to proposing to existing clients vary from sector to sector. In advertising and marketing services businesses, the request for a re-pitch is nearly always construed as a prelude to losing the account, and as a result the invitation will often be declined. The remarks below from two senior executives within the industry are typical:

> We won't do it. If things have got to the stage where you're asked to re-pitch, it's likely that, for whatever reason, the relationship has deteriorated to the point where you stand very little chance of being re-appointed. There's also a personal disinclination to do it; I put in a lot of personal effort with clients, and I'm disappointed if they want to start looking at other advisers.

> We very rarely do it. The chances of winning in a formal pitch are pretty low. We never used to re-pitch at all but, these days, it's become a more legitimate thing to ask for although, personally, I tend to see it negatively – more than I should, probably. One gets very personally involved, and one's pride is hurt.

In contrast, it is not unusual for accounting firms, and to an increasing extent law firms, to be asked to participate in a formal competitive proposal by an existing client; and in nearly all cases they will agree to do so. Except where there has been an horrendous error or a complete breakdown in communication – in which case the incumbent is unlikely to be on the shortlist – the firm may stand a good chance of retaining the business. Certainly, there have been a number of occasions where this has happened.

There are two explanations for this difference in attitude. The clients of lawyers and accountants will probably have originally appointed their advisers without recourse to a formal proposal, as this requirement is still a comparatively recent phenomenon. Putting advisers through a proposal process may often therefore be interpreted as a desire to conform with current best practice, rather than as an expression of dissatisfaction with their performance. Marketing services companies, on the other hand, will have had to pitch to get the work in the first place. The other explanation lies in the importance which is generally attached to continuity in the provision of accounting and legal services. An incumbent can always argue that, as it knows the client best, it can provide the service most efficiently and with the minimum disruption. In the marketing services sector, rather more emphasis tends to be placed on fresh thinking, and rather less on continuity.

As the second quotation above suggests, proposal activity is generally on the increase and it is likely that more companies in the future will ask for incumbents to re-propose as a matter of course. Advisers should, perhaps, have a better reason than hurt pride to decline the invitation.

Making your decision

Work through the factors listed above, and decide whether any might present problems. Some service providers insist that rigorous criteria must be satisfied before they will agree to participate. According to a director of a leading merchant bank:

> Apart from being sure that the job will be profitable and that we can staff it, we only get involved if we have a better than even chance of winning. We have no compunction in rejecting an invitation to tender if it doesn't meet our criteria. It's not going to harm our reputation, and we can't afford to devote time to flimsy opportunities.

Perhaps this is the right approach for a leading merchant bank, but few of us can afford to be so cavalier: the decision to decline an invitation should not be taken lightly, especially if the organisation which has asked you to propose is potentially of strategic importance to your firm. The proposal process can be an outstanding way to develop a business relationship – worth more than a hundred cocktail parties. And even if you don't win, a good performance may put you in the frame for other work which the organisation has to offer.

PRE-EMPTIVE TACTICS

Before you actually make your response to an invitation, it is worth pausing to ascertain if there is any way in which the proposal arrangements can be pre-empted.

We have said that a formal competitive tender is a time-consuming and expensive process: take, for example, the case of the US advertising agency Chiat/Day. Newspaper reports estimated that the agency spent $1 million on out of pocket expenses to win the Nissan account (worth $150 million in annual billings). But it is not just advertising agencies which spend a fortune on the pursuit of new business. Insurance brokers, auditors and other service providers are often required to make a huge investment in terms of the time costs of their senior people, especially for worldwide assignments. Although there have been some instances where contenders have been paid a fee to put their proposal together (such as in the advertising and design industries), we can assume that the fee would not have made much of a dent on the actual costs of the exercise; and such instances have in any case been few and far between.

The costs of proposing might be easier to accept if the outcome were more predictable. In the majority of cases, however, you will have the feeling that you are being asked to make a guaranteed investment in exchange for a most uncertain return. The number of contenders invited to participate in a competitive proposal varies enormously. But on average, with all other things being equal, your chances of winning are unlikely to exceed 20 per cent.

Seen in this light, being asked to propose could even be regarded as a failure: is there no other, more efficient way you could have secured the business? Even if the answer is yes, by the time you receive the invitation it will probably be too late to do anything about it. This underlines the critical role that targeting has to play in the marketing mix. An effective targeting campaign not only puts you in pole position once the invitation to tender has been issued; it may even give you the chance to pre-empt the process altogether. It is instructive in this context to look at how merchant banks generate new business opportunities. According to one New York-based ex-investment banker:

> First, we determine from a company's public financial statements what the company needs – say a preferred stock issue. Then we make an appointment to see the chief financial officer and say: 'we think your company could really benefit from this for these reasons . . .' and state them. We round it off by saying 'We brought you this idea and we'd like you to retain us to do this piece of business'. It's a highly speculative approach, but based on thorough analysis. A great deal of work will have been done on putting together a cogent argument for why this particular product fits a specific need which the company has. The message is twofold: this is the best product to fit your need, and we are the best people to make it happen. This is common practice in corporate America: companies expect investment bankers to come in periodically and make presentations on specific ideas.

Such an approach is not replicable in all business sectors, of course, but it does provide a useful illustration of how the speculative investment of time and energy in a new business proposition can actually save time by pre-empting a competitive process later on.

Once a formal brief has been distributed to a number of prospective suppliers, your chances of derailing the process are negligible. There may be occasions, however, when you are given the chance to talk to a potential client before other contenders for the work get involved. Gambits intended to dissuade the organisation from pressing ahead with the process must naturally be essayed with considerable subtlety. The three methods most likely to succeed are:

(i)   suggesting that any cost savings achieved by putting a service out to tender may be negated by the disruption and cost (to management) of the tender itself; and that the offer from your firm to discount significantly if the tender is abandoned will enable the organisation to achieve the best of both worlds – a lower price and no disruption. Where the organisation is contemplating a tender in order to ensure that it achieves a competitive price – and is seen to be achieving it by, for example, outside shareholders – it may be helpful to offer to conduct a 'benchmarking' exercise. This might involve providing details of fees charged to similar clients, showing how the costs sub-divide between various activities; or developing a set of criteria by which the achievement of a 'fair' price can be judged.

(ii)   suggesting that proposing is by nature a rather artificial exercise, that primarily tests the suppliers' ability to perform well during the selection process, rather than their ability to do the actual job. (Generations of schoolchildren have surely used a similar logic in attempting to evade the horrors of the formal examination.) Not everyone is sold on the idea that a formal tendering process is the best way to select advisers. The legal director of one of the UK's largest companies had this to say about selecting outside firms of solicitors to do high-level corporate finance work: 'In corporate finance, you are buying the lawyers' problem-solving ability: it is an iterative process. How could you possibly ascertain this from a beauty parade?' You might put forward the idea that the prospective client would get greater value from a different kind of exercise; you might, for example, propose to under-take a small job – let's say a 'preliminary study' or 'diagnostic review' – without charge. This may appeal to the prospective client as a way of finding out what you are capable of, without having to make a commitment; and it is likely to pre-empt the involvement of other potential contenders.

(iii) offering to help the prospective client plan and organise the tendering process, with a view either to achieving an unassailable advantage over the other firms, or even per-suading the organisation that a tender is unnecessary. A marketing services firm, for example, has benefited on a number of occasions from helping a prospective client pre-pare the proposal brief:

If the organisation cannot supply a proper brief, we may help them do it. There are instances where we've helped to get the brief right to the extent that they haven't bothered with the pitch; the penny drops that they don't actually have to ask these questions of any other company.

Your best chance to use these techniques may well arise when you are the incumbent. To start with, assuming that the relationship is reasonably healthy, you are likely to get advanced warning that a proposal process is being considered; that gives you time to think how you might deflect the client from his intentions. Find out why your contract is under review and respond accordingly, for example by offering to identify cost savings (an instant offer to cut the price may look like panic) or by replacing a member of the team. In the public sector, there is often a concern that suppliers develop too cosy a relationship with departments if working with them over long periods; and consequently, there may be pressure for assignments to be rotated among different suppliers. In these circumstances, you might offer to develop a proposal *before* the service is put out to tender, showing that your price is still competitive and that in providing the service you have retained your objectivity.

Other opportunities to deploy these methods will be limited. But it is worth bearing in mind that some organisations do not want the disruption of a tendering process, or possibly are even a little frightened of it, but feel obliged all the same to conduct one. Your suggesting alternatives in such circumstances might be welcomed with open arms.

MAKING YOUR RESPONSE

You need to react quickly once an invitation is received; do not sit on it while you think about the numerous imponderables raised in this chapter. A slow response may be interpreted as lack of interest, or poor organisation, or both. In order to decide how (or whether) you will participate, you should try to extract as much information as possible from the prospective client. Things you will need to find out include:

- precise nature and scope of the assignment
- how the service is currently provided (e.g. external supplier or in-house department); if external, name of the incumbent
- the formal outputs of the process, e.g. preliminary interviews, proposal document, presentation
- the timetable for the above
- the motivations behind the tender, e.g. dissatisfaction with current suppliers, need to reduce costs, desire to move from fixed cost to variable cost (in the case of outsourcing), need to improve quality of existing service, an entirely new requirement, or some combination of these
- the criteria by which the successful contender will be selected
- budget available for the assignment, and current spend (where applicable)
- whether further information on the company is available (background papers, strategy documents etc)
- attitudes to contenders having potential conflicts of interest, and whether these will disqualify them from participating
- whether the assignment may carry any business risks for your firm (e.g. relating to contractual obligations)
- why your firm has been included on the shortlist
- the names of other firms which have been asked to participate
- who you are allowed to contact within the organisation as part of the tender process.

Many of these points will be covered if you have received a written brief, but there is always scope to ask further questions. For example, the brief may state that the successful firm 'must have a track record in the area of the assignment and the resources to be able to carry it out'. It goes without saying that you should be able to develop a more detailed picture of the selection criteria if you talk it over with the nominated contact within the tendering organisation.

A light touch is needed at this stage of the proposal process. Do not send a list of questions seeking further information: you are trying to read between the lines as well as on them, and a little gentle probing is likely to reveal much more than just the mechanics of the process. Use the 'phone. If there is no existing relationship between the organisation and your firm, the 'phone enables you to start one. From this initial contact you may begin to gauge its style and culture: whether, for example, it is hierarchical or egalitarian, ruthlessly profit-driven or paternalistic. Armed with a first impression, you can begin to lay the foundations of a winning strategy.

KEY POINTS

- The campaign starts the moment you receive the invitation to tender; the potential client will be watching and assessing your firm from the very beginning of the process.

- If you are requested to send credentials, try to tailor your response to the potential client rather than submitting standard corporate material.

- Consider the form and context in which the invitation has arisen; make a dispassionate assessment of how and why the tender has come about, and what this tells you about your chances of success.

- Incumbents asked to re-propose must make an honest appraisal of where they stand and whether to accept, but no firm should decline an invitation solely because of injured pride.

- Assess the sincerity of the invitation; warning signs include large pitch lists, the absence of a brief, vagueness about the process, reluctance to set up a meeting and evasiveness over budgets.

- In deciding whether to accept, make a thorough assessment of the costs and benefits of proposing, the likely profitability of the assignment, availability of resources, and if there are any unacceptable business risks.

- Never decline an invitation to tender for non-commercial reasons; even where the likelihood of success is remote, your participation may pay significant dividends over the long term.

- Where you have advance notice of a tender, consider whether you can pre-empt the process by suggesting alternatives to the target organisation, such as offering to conduct a preliminary study or to promise a discount for abandoning the process.

- Respond promptly to all invitations to tender; delays will convey a lack of interest and poor organisation.

- Where no personal relationship exists with the potential client, establish one by discussing the brief with your nominated contact within the organisation.

- Where possible, use the acceptance process to begin clarifying the organisation's needs and extracting information – never send a list of questions.

3

LAYING THE FOUNDATIONS FOR SUCCESS

THE MANAGEMENT IMPERATIVE

The development of a winning proposal requires more than thorough research and creative commercial thinking. Critical as these things are, a brilliant strategy will not help you win the business if the document arrives a week later than it was supposed to; management and logistics are just as important to the outcome. Different sectors set tenderers different timescales: an auditor may get two or three months in which to develop his proposal; an investment banker, on the other hand, may be given only two or three weeks. Whether the timescale is long or short, there is no excuse for not having made clear within your own organisation who needs to do what and by which date. And that means strong proposal management skills.

Furthermore, the overall impression created by how you manage the proposal process is critical. The reason is neatly summed up by the finance director of a large UK company:

> The winning practice got it right from the first day. They stuck to the schedule, made the right follow-ups, spent their time with us sensibly and did everything they said they were going to do on time. It augured well for the audit.

THE PROPOSAL LEADER

The successful development of a winning strategy calls for strong leadership – nothing, in fact, is more fundamental to the success of your tender. There are many reasons for this.

Why leadership matters

Like most other areas of commercial activity, proposal development by committee is unlikely to achieve the best results. Of course there should be consultation and discussion with colleagues – not least because they may have a very detailed knowledge of or inside track on the prospective client which the leader lacks – but this does not mean there has to be consensus on every issue.

When the pressure mounts near the end, only one person can take the final decision where there are conflicting views on, say, the proposed fee or the structure of the document. This is particularly apposite in the context of professional partnerships, where everyone tends to feel obliged to consult everyone else and, worse still, act on their comments.

The basic rule is: don't govern the process by decree, but don't worry about incorporating all your colleagues' views either. The line has to be drawn somewhere.

More importantly, the potential client will want to see leadership vested in a single person. Whatever the project or relationship you are proposing for, the target organisation will usually look to one individual to carry overall responsibility for the services being provided. A leader who is reluctant to take decisions during the proposal process is unlikely to prove very effective if he or she is awarded the contract.

Is it possible, however, to assign leadership of the proposal process to one person and the ultimate leadership of the team when the job has been won to someone else? This way (so the argument runs), you can make the most of people whose selling skills are stronger than their ability to keep a project on track once it has been awarded.

Don't be persuaded by this line of thinking. For the reason just mentioned, leadership demonstrated in the proposal process will be regarded by the potential client as a concrete indication of how effectively the individual will perform if given the assignment. Any other arrangement is likely to be perceived as a cynical attempt to win the business – and nothing more. (See the following chapter on the dangers of deploying a figurehead or proposal 'expert' in this role.)

Selecting the proposal leader

Leaving aside all the questions of personality match, relevant experience and so on, how can you make sure that you have selected the right person?

The question is often answered for you – most usually because it is the recipient of the letter of invitation whom the potential client wants to propose for his business. Whether this is always the best policy is a moot point; he or she may have a personal contact within the target organisation, which is why the invitation to tender has been sent to them. This does not, of course, mean that this person has either the right skills or temperament to lead the proposal team.

Again, the issue tends to cause the greatest problems in professional practices, where partners have traditionally been reluctant to pass on the opportunity of proposing for new and potentially lucrative work to their colleagues. After all, money talks, and no-one likes to give up the chance of acquiring more chargeable hours on their timesheet. A separate book could be written about this issue but, at the very least, give the matter some careful thought; the person who receives the invitation does not have an automatic right to lead the proposal team.

Self-selecting or not, it is imperative that the nominated proposal leader has sufficient time to devote to the task. The proposal must take priority over all other commitments. Anything else is a recipe for weak management, poor coordination and, most probably, failure. If you are unable to delegate your duties to others, don't take the job on.

What are the personal qualities you should expect from a proposal leader? However you choose to define them, it is almost certain that there will not be as many people in your firm with the requisite attributes as you would like. But it will help to have a profile of the ideal candidate in your mind before deciding who is likely to be the best choice.

Of course, the proposal leader must be credible in the eyes of the potential client; he or she must therefore have personal authority, preferably backed up with convincing credentials and an impressive track record on similar assignments. Leaders must be persuasive, enthusiastic, and able to convey the notion that they have a genuine desire to help the prospective client – not just in the interests of winning or retaining the work, but because they are focused on finding solutions and helping to achieve their clients' objectives.

As your knowledge of the prospective client will in many cases be limited, the leader must have the ability to see beyond the facts which are available, and draw the right conclusions. He or she will need to understand the motivations of the decision-makers, and the factors which will weigh most heavily when making their choice: not only those which have been alluded to in the brief, but also the more subjective and personal issues which are at least as important. In any competitive tender, powers of observation and perspicacity are at a premium.

So are management skills. For the reasons already discussed, the proposal leader must have the ability to take decisions and arbitrate between conflicting views among the team – explaining how and why the assignment can be won and what individual team members need to do to help achieve that goal. If there is one quality which sums up what is most needed of the proposal leader it is *vision*; the vision to understand what the prospective client really wants and the vision to formulate the best solution.

The role of the proposal leader

In addition to bearing ultimate responsibility for the management of the proposal process, the team leader needs to address a variety of key areas both in the planning stage and as the proposal develops.

One of the most important planning issues is budgets. Proposals can consume vast amounts of time and money and, as we said in the previous chapter, the level of resources expended on the exercise must be linked to the potential revenue likely to be gained. Unfortunately, there is no definitive formula for assessing how much you should spend, especially when the value of the assignment may be difficult to quantify.

Obviously, however, there is no point in incurring document production costs of £10,000 on a once-only project with a fee of £5,000 (which may seem obvious, but there are any number of instances where this kind of profligacy has occurred). Difficult as the budgetary aspect sometimes is, the issue needs to be tackled early on. Always maintain a commercial perspective on the tender; the excitement and momentum of the process can often result in proposals assuming a life of their own, where the cost is totally out of proportion to the potential financial benefit.

The proposal leader also needs to think about how his or her resources can be most effectively marshalled to develop a winning strategy. That means assembling the appropriate research material and personnel, and thinking about what kind of information is required. It also means identifying colleagues and others (such as consultants) who can help in the development of the strategy, the writing of the document or in preparing the team for the presentation.

Another key responsibility is briefing the team. Everyone needs to have the clearest possible idea of what role they are being asked to perform. When time is in short supply – as it always seems to be in proposal situations – it is imperative that there is no duplication of effort and that the endeavours of each individual complement rather than conflict with those of their colleagues. This is especially critical during the interview stage, where clear and discrete lines of questioning need to be assigned to each person involved. Few things alienate a prospective client faster than being asked the same question twice.

Before you can reach that stage, however, you need to have selected the team. This is the proposal leader's first important job; the way he or she manages that team throughout the process will be key to the success of the proposal.

In putting the team together, there is inevitably a temptation to use people you know, like and are used to working with. But, as with all proposals activity, the obvious route is not always the most effective. These individuals may not be appropriate for any number of reasons: they may not have the right level of experience; they may lack expertise in the potential client's industry sector; or, most basic of all, they may not be the sort of people which the potential client can get on with – even if you can. The difficult decisions about team composition should always rest with the proposal leader. Again, if the team leader does not want to risk upsetting his colleagues, he should not volunteer for the job.

MANAGING THE PROPOSAL PROCESS

Even if, as we recommend in the next chapter, the proposal leader delegates the day-to-day running of the proposal, this will not obviate the need for highly developed management skills. Part of the leader's job is to ensure that the team stays motivated through-out the exercise, and that those responsible for various aspects of the process do not lose sight of the objectives. Each member of the team should be kept informed as the proposal progresses, and have an opportunity to contribute to the development of the strategy. At the same time, the proposal leader must stay firmly in control and be seen to be setting the direction of the process. Within these general themes, the proposal leader needs to bear in mind some specific points about the management of the exercise.

Critical path analysis

The critical path analysis is a key tool in ensuring that the process is managed effectively. Fig. 3.1 sets out a critical path for a major multinational tender, constructed by working backwards from the date of the oral presentation. It is essentially a timetable with deadlines, telling you at a glance where the tender has reached at any particular moment, and how you expect the proposal to develop in the remaining time available.

The critical path should be prepared as soon as possible after you have received the invitation to tender. That way, everyone in your team will know what they have to do and the date by which they have to complete it.

Liaison with the target organisation

All your meetings and other contact with the potential client in the run-up to the presentation should be coordinated by the proposal leader. The focus and direction of these meetings need to be strictly controlled, since the conduct of your team, and the impression made by its members, will be central to the final outcome.

Liaison with other teams

Significant tenders issued by large international companies will often require the involvement of several proposal teams from different territories. Where you need to bring in overseas offices – or outside contractors – as part of your proposal, it is vital that their efforts are carefully coordinated. The proposal leader needs to take full and direct responsibility for making sure that this happens; if each team takes a different approach, the results will convey a poor impression of your firm's ability to organise and manage resources.

Where a large project is involved, prospective clients will often want to be reassured about your ability to manage work across several territories. These concerns need to be tackled head on:

Week no	1	2	3	4	5	6	7	8
Month	MARCH			APRIL				MAY
Week beginning	15th	22nd	27th	5th	12th	19th	26th	3rd
CENTRAL TEAM – London	17th Brainstorming 18th Desk research 18th Brief star teams	23rd Brief designers ← SITE VISITS	1st Agree design VISITS	5th Brainstorming 7th Circulate Draft 1 9th Circulate Draft 2	12th Plan Presentation 13th Circulate Draft 3 18th Draft to Panel	19th Agree Final draft 20th Documents to printers	26th Submit Documents 29th Rehearsal 30th Full Rehearsal	3rd Full dress rehearsal 4th Presentation
UK DIVISIONAL TEAMS – Birmingham – Edinburgh			2nd Feedback to London →				25th Local team leader arrives London	
INTERNATIONAL TEAMS – Chicago – Frankfurt – Singapore – Sydney			2nd Feedback to London →				29th Local Team leaders depart for London	
PROPOSALS PANEL – London	18th Brief Panel			5th Discuss approach with panel	16th Review Draft 4		30th Review presentation	3rd Review Presentation

Figure 3.1 Critical path analysis

We were not convinced of the team's ability to coordinate service delivery through their organisation's international network, in terms of either quality or timeliness.

Avoiding this kind of criticism calls for effective briefing and liaison, and making clear how your lines of international communication will operate in practice. It may also require you to bring in overseas colleagues on some of the key site visits to show that, when you discuss international experience and integrated resources, your claims are genuine.

The proposal leader will need to have the final say on issues such as pricing and the composition of teams being put forward elsewhere. And again, it is up to the proposal leader to ensure that each 'remote' team is fully briefed before any contact is made with the potential client's local operations. They must have a firm grasp of the issues which need be explored and the key messages which your firm wishes to convey.

These issues might include the way in which each of the potential client's international operations liaise with and report to group headquarters. What are their information requirements, reporting deadlines and other time constraints? Where are their weaknesses in terms of personnel or systems in complying with group structures? What do the overseas managers need from their local advisers in order to achieve group objectives? As with the key messages, you might need to emphasise the strength of your own firm's international communications channels and your commitment to universal standards of service quality. You may also need to reassure local decision-makers that you can marshal the necessary resources and skills from other territories to provide specialist assistance on ad hoc assignments.

When asked for their views by the centre, you want the overseas operations of the potential client to confirm that the favourable impression your firm has made at group level is replicated in their own countries. Making sure that happens is a question of good team selection, clear briefing and effective communication.

Handling large tenders

The principles which underpin successful proposal management apply with equal force whether a tender is small or large, and has a long or a short lead time. There are, however, subtle differences which you need to take into account.

In the case of a large proposal, your planning will have to be meticulous. You may be required to manage the activities of several proposal teams at the same time, and to deal with a large number of site visits to many different subsidiaries of the potential client. The production side of the process is also likely to be more elaborate and therefore time-consuming; the written submission, for instance, may need to comprise separate documents for each subsidiary.

Far more challenging is the need to decipher the larger organisation's politics and decision-making processes. The bigger the organisation, the harder it is to work out who really matters. At first sight, it may not be obvious who the key decision-makers are, and the person who sent you the invitation to tender may have comparatively little influence on the final decision. Getting to grips with whose opinions count requires careful probing.

Smaller proposals

These problems are unlikely to occur where the prospective client is an owner-managed business or, for that matter, a small part of a large organisation. It will usually be obvious who the key decision-makers are.

In the case of an owner-managed business, a proposal which contains strong commercial ideas is always more likely to pay greater dividends than one which merely outlines your experience and credentials. An owner-manager whose personal circumstances are inextricably linked with the success of his business needs to feel confident that his advisers will contribute something to the way the enterprise is run, and not simply fulfil a series of technical requirements.

Where you may be proposing for a small subsidiary or department, bear in mind that the people deciding on your tender may have to explain why they want to appoint you to others in the parent company or central office. Give some thought, therefore, to the kinds of messages they will want to hear in your proposal, even if the necessary approval process is largely a question of rubber-stamping.

Last-minute proposals

Where you may be given only a few days to respond to an invitation to tender, a critical path analysis will be even more important. If a formal proposal document is required, it should still be possible to produce something which is structured effectively and looks professional. This can be achieved, for example, by dropping in the prospective client's logo on pre-printed covers and using a word-processor which can print a variety of typefaces (as most will nowadays).

IDENTIFYING THE INGREDIENTS FOR SUCCESS

While the logistics of the proposal are critical, you and everyone else in your team must maintain a clear focus on the main objective: to win the work by devising a more compelling proposition than any of your competitors. That means an efficiently organised process, the right team and, above all, as precise an understanding as possible of the potential client's business, needs, objectives and ambitions.

How should you begin to get to grips with what the target organisation needs and wants to achieve?

Brainstorming

The first step is a brainstorming session, attended by the whole team. This is a vital meeting at which everyone should be

encouraged to air their initial ideas on the invitation to tender –
however rough and ready they may be. The more you discuss it, the
better your proposal is likely to be.

The session should be used to raise key questions and, later on,
to begin developing some central themes. The questions might
include:

- why has the prospective client asked us to tender?
- what do we already know about their organisation and key
  decision-makers, and where do we need to find out more?
- what are they likely to be looking for from our proposal?
- who will our competitors be – and why have they been asked to
  tender?
- should we follow the letter of their brief, or adopt a more
  ambitious approach?

The last of these marks the stage when you start to develop your
proposition for winning the business. Make sure, though, that you
have found out as many answers as you can to the preceding
questions before you tackle this one. The most imaginative proposal in the world will come to nothing if you have ignored what the
prospective client orginally asked for. This is not to say you cannot
reinterpret or expand on the tender brief if you feel it will pay
dividends – what clients say they want is rarely all that they need.
But you must tackle the issues which you have been asked to
address; responding only to the brief which you think the decision-
makers *should* have written will considerably lengthen the odds
against your winning.

It would be unlikely, of course, if any member of your proposal
team entering the first brainstorming session did not already have
an idea about the approach you should be taking. This is particularly true of the proposal leader, who will probably have had the
longest time in which to consider the invitation and therefore to
form an initial opinion.

The risk is that the leader may use the meeting to expound his or
her preferred approach, and the brainstorming degenerates into a
series of instructions to the rest of the team to find the evidence or

information which supports that theory. Meetings like this are worse than useless, and reinforce the need to choose your proposal leader very carefully. More than any other, this particular session should give the freest possible rein to those present so that every idea, however inchoate or unorthodox, can be heard and discussed.

Later on as time presses and the team learns more about what is and is not likely to produce results, the meetings will require more structure and focus. But at the first brainstorming, everyone should put their preconceptions aside, and be ready to listen, debate and contribute.

Critical success factors matrix

An important tool for making sure you head in the most productive direction – and, in particular, for knowing what to look out for in the site visits – is shown in Fig. 3.2. This particular example sets out the sort of issues which a large firm of lawyers might need to consider when tendering for an international assignment.

The best time to draw up the matrix is immediately after your initial brainstorming. It will act as a summary of the issues you have discussed, and provide a 'road map' for your site visits and other lines of enquiry. However artificial the scoring might be, the matrix will play an important part in helping to develop your approach. It will assist you in crystallising your thinking about the prospective client and what more you need to find out. It will also highlight areas where your firm is ahead or behind the competition, show where information is weak or unreliable, and provide an indication of which issues should be given prominence in your proposal.

The matrix should not, however, be set in stone. It needs to be revisited at every subsequent team meeting so that the gaps can be filled in and new issues added as soon as you become aware of them. The scoring is therefore also likely to change; if it doesn't, it is a sure sign that your understanding of the target organisation and the context in which the proposal is taking place has not progressed very far.

Critical success	Your firm	Competitor A	Competitor B
Business issues Ability to understand the key issues and contribute value – eg in the areas of: * commercial objectives * managing legal risk * anti-trust implications * other key issues			
Resources and credentials Strengths in terms of: * quality of the team * industry expertise * relevant experience * geographical coverage * existing credibility with potential client * firm's general reputation			
Managing the assignment Ability to provide: * leadership * specialist advice * effective fee management * right balance of senior and junior time * continuity			
Political issues Grasp of: * who the key decision-makers are * sensitivities of individual directors * existing allegiances/ sympathies			

Figure 3.2 Critical success factors matrix

For each issue, estimate your own and your competitors' strengths, and grade them between 1 and 5 (1 = strong; 5 = weak).

FORMULATING RESEARCH OBJECTIVES

The critical success factors matrix will be helpful in setting your research objectives – as will, of course, the invitation to tender. In your initial brainstorming session, draw up a list of the things you need to find out about the prospective client, your competitors and – often overlooked – yourselves. Then ask some key questions.

Personalities

What are the people to whom you are proposing actually like? What kind of attributes do they admire in their advisers or suppliers and, conversely, which do they dislike? The answers will be central to deciding which members of your team should be given prominent roles and, indeed, how you should approach the proposal document. Do the decision-makers like detail or prefer a broader overview? Are they patient people who are likely to read and compare documents very thoroughly, or do they find it easier to absorb short, sharp messages which can be assimilated more quickly?

The people who will decide

Who will actually take the decision on your proposal? As we said earlier, the person who signed the letter of invitation may have very little influence on who gets the job. The 'public' hierarchy of the organisation can also be misleading; the person who really matters – or will influence those who 'officially' take the decision – may not even be on the Board. He or she could, for instance, be a personal assistant to the chief executive who has been charged with reviewing and making recommendations on each submission. Unless you find out who is assessing your tender, you may spend the entire process courting someone who is either indifferent to or incapable of influencing the final decision.

Concerns and ambitions

When you have found out who the real decision-makers are, you will need to gain a clearer picture of their interests and objectives. What do they want their organisation to achieve, and what are their concerns? What kind of help do they need in making the most of their own skills, and how can you provide that help without exposing their weaknesses?

Culture and management style

Some of the answers to these questions are likely to be suggested by the type of organisation to which the decision-makers belong. Is it a management culture which encourages caution, or does the company welcome the challenge of new thinking and radical action? Does it thrive on change and innovation, or prefer to maintain the status quo? However arcane, every organisation has a corporate culture with a set of values to which your approach to site visits, the written submission and oral presentation needs to be sensitive.

Your perceived role

What are the decision-makers hoping to achieve through the tender? They may have asked everyone to tender according to the same brief but, as we said in Chapter 2, it could be that this is merely a set of minimum requirements on which they want proposers to build. How much added value are they looking for, or do they genuinely want you to do only what they have specified and nothing more?

The potential client's strengths and weaknesses

What are the strengths and weaknesses of the target organisation? What opportunities does it need to seize and, conversely, what is it threatened by? How does what the organisation says about itself in its annual report or brochures compare with information from independent sources? How is the organisation positioned in its marketplace, and what effect will new or imminent developments in the sector have?

Your own strengths and weaknesses

Look at your own firm in a similar way. To what extent do your strengths and weaknesses affect your ability to help the organisation address theirs? In what areas of activity is it likely to have a favourable or unfavourable impression of your firm?

The tender itself

Why has the organisation put its requirements out to tender? Many prospective clients' briefs fail to address the subject, and it is surprising how often proposers also neglect to pursue the issue. Was it dissatisfaction with current arrangements, or simply a matter of policy? The answer can tell you a good deal about the approach you should be taking, and the kind of competition you can expect.

Your competitors

Who are your competitors, and why has the target organisation asked them to tender? Again, many proposers brush over the issue, either because they feel they can't ask the question, or because other firms are considered a known quantity. Since a successful proposal is all about creating differentiation from your competitors, it is imperative to find out who you are competing against, and how your respective strengths and weaknesses compare in the context of this particular tender.

When you start getting some answers, go back to the critical success factors matrix which you drew up in your initial brainstorming session. See how the issues and your relative strengths have changed in the light of your findings, and amend your approach accordingly.

TACKLING DEFENSIVE PROPOSALS

Do any of these principles and techniques apply when you are required to develop possibly the most difficult proposal of all – the one in which you have been asked to tender for reappointment?

They all do. Having considered the issues outlined in the previous chapter and decided that the tender is worth pursuing, try to put to one side your preconceptions about the client organisation and, in particular, any feelings of damaged pride. Imagine instead that you are proposing to an organisation with which you have had no previous dealings.

Think hard about why you have been asked to re-tender. Have you made mistakes in the past, or is it your fee structure they object to? Has the organisation been acquired by another which wants to rationalise the number of advisers or suppliers? The answers may be considerably more prosaic than you think – very few organisations are keen to embark on a disruptive tendering process and change of advisers simply because they feel vindictive towards the incumbent and just want to waste your time. If they disliked your firm that much, you would not have been asked to re-tender.

Even if you feel you know the organisation backwards, do not pass up the opportunity of site visits because you think there is nothing new to say. Use them to discuss how needs have changed and to probe the client about the approach being taken by your competitors. Set out your findings in a critical success factors matrix just as you would for any other proposal.

Define the benefits you have been able to deliver in the past, and highlight constructive contributions made to the client's business. If pricing is the issue, analyse costs and show how they have remained competitive against those charged by others in your sector; if they have risen sharply, explain why – perhaps, for instance, because of inefficiencies or mistakes made within the client organisation itself.

But be careful how you tackle this. This is what the recently appointed finance director of a UK company had to say about an incumbent firm of auditors attempting to justify mounting fees:

They sought to explain their rising costs on inefficiencies in the audit due to me – in a private letter to the managing director. Leaving aside the crass attempt to go over my head, it ignored the fact that their fees had risen significantly long before I arrived at the company.

Whatever you find out from your interviews and site visits, do not assume that you can carry on as you did before. By definition, something has gone wrong somewhere in the relationship, and you will need to suggest a fresh approach and some new ideas.

If there have been management changes in the client organisation, do what you can to get closer to the new people. If there have been changes in your own team, analyse what effect these may have had within the client organisation or on the efficiency of your own working practices. Alternatively, if there have been no changes, you may need to inject some new blood. Think, too, about whether *you* may be part of the problem, and whether the greater good would be served by putting forward a colleague in your place. The same finance director mentioned above had this to say about the incumbent client service partner:

> Too much water had gone under the bridge for me and the lead partner to continue working together. Their tax partner and audit manager were actually very good, and if they'd only replaced the audit partner with someone else, the firm would have stood a very good chance of being reappointed.

Whatever you do, do not just repeat your credentials – use what you know about the client. You would rather that the client doesn't dismiss your proposal in this way:

> The incumbent firm knew our strengths and weaknesses, and had the inside track. But they didn't raise any of these issues during the site visits or in their document; they knew what we're like as an organisation, but failed to use or develop their knowledge.

It is better not to knock the competition, however genuinely you believe they may not be up to the job. Demonstrate instead your in-depth knowledge of the business, emphasising how you will use this to meet changing needs and build on the benefits delivered in the past. As this suggests, it is vital that your proposal looks to the future, not solely to the past. Form a clear grasp of why your reappointment has not been a formality, and act on your findings as constructively as you can. Make an honest assessment of past weaknesses, followed by a clear statement of how things will improve. This is always more effective than thinking you can gloss over the problem:

> If they had told us how and why their approach had changed, done a critique of the relationship and their historical approach, that would have altered our view considerably.

Above all, don't lose heart. Remember that unlike your competitors, you are the only proposer who can offer the client the combination of continuity *and* a new approach.

KEY POINTS

- The individual who receives the invitation should not automatically be given leadership of the proposal team; he must have the relevant technical expertise, experience, management skills and, above all, the vision to understand and assess the organisation's needs.

- The leader of the proposal team must give the task priority over all other commitments.

- The team leader should act as the final arbiter on team selection and any differences of opinion about the firm's approach; he should also coordinate all contact with the prospective client, and monitor costs to ensure they remain in proportion to the potential financial benefit.

- The proposal leader must be seen to be taking a full and active part throughout the proposal process; he cannot be perceived by the potential client as a figurehead whose involvement is designed only to win the assignment.

- Give each member of the proposal team a clear brief so that they know precisely what their individual tasks and objectives are.

- Draw up a critical path analysis which allows sufficient time for discussion, feedback, contributions from any other teams involved, and the practical aspects of document production and presentation preparation.

- Organise a first brainstorming session for the proposal team at which everyone is encouraged to air initial ideas about how to approach the proposal.

- Develop a critical success factors matrix to help determine research objectives, and in which an honest assessment is made of your strengths and weaknesses in relation to competitors; revisit and revise the matrix at every subsequent team meeting.

- Identify the key questions about the potential client's needs and circumstances: these should take account of the personalities, concerns and ambitions of the people to whom you are proposing; and the management style, corporate culture and commercial objectives of the organisation.

- Approach a defensive proposal as you would any other, but be objective about your shortcomings and look to the future.

4

CHOOSING THE RIGHT TEAM

THE SIGNIFICANCE OF THE TEAM

'People buy people, not firms. Few would take issue with this well-worn aphorism. Buying and selling is usually a personal business, whatever trade is being engaged in. It applies to commodities or manufactured goods, as well as to services. The private consumer and corporate decision-maker alike can be as influenced by the personal qualities of a salesman as the technical attributes of his product.

There are, however, particular reasons why the team is likely to be one of the key factors in a proposal. The purchaser is usually buying two things through this process: a set of skills or capacities which, for any number of reasons, have to be resourced externally; and a working relationship. The success of that relationship will often determine the effectiveness of the purchase. Put another way, the purchaser is buying both a *product* – capabilities, expertise or experience; and a *service* – the manner in which the product is provided, and how the provider intends to manage the relationship with the client. Both the product and the service, of course, depend to a great extent on the people who are assigned to the engagement.

In fact, understanding the distinction between the two is critical to formulating a successful proposal strategy. This is because the prospective purchaser – consciously or unconsciously – moves through a two-stage process in selecting his suppliers or advisers;

contenders need to be aware of which stage the prospective client has reached and how this affects the criteria by which they are assessed.

He first has to decide which contenders are capable of meeting his requirements: a decision which will rest on his assessment of their skills and expertise, their track record on similar projects, and their depth and breadth of resources.

He will then have to decide which contender he actually wants to work with. This is bound to involve a more subjective assessment – which team inspires the most confidence? Which is likely to be the most stimulating to work with? Which demonstrates the greatest empathy with what the client is trying to achieve? Which is likely to be able to handle unforeseen problems quickly and efficiently? Which set of individuals does the client actually *like* the most?

The answers to these questions will obviously be crucial to the outcome, and together are often described as 'personal chemistry'. As we shall see, chemistry – in so far as it conjures up an image of an intrinsic personal rapport which cannot be altered or enhanced through conscious effort – is a rather unhelpful idea. Proposers may not be able to affect whether they are liked by the potential client; in the early stages of the contest, he is in any case unlikely to have a strong view one way or the other. But they can consciously influence, for example, his perception of their understanding of his needs, whether or not they will be stimulating to work with and whether or not they inspire confidence. This we will return to later. For the moment, the important point is that the purchaser must be convinced both that a team is capable of doing the job *and* that he wants to work with it.

This two-stage buying process has been described by David H Maister, the former Harvard Business School professor, as 'qualification' and 'selection' ('How clients choose', in *Managing the Professional Service Firm*, Free Press, 1993). Sometimes, the distinction is made explicit by the purchaser, who conducts what is misleadingly called a 'pre-qualification' stage intended to create a shortlist from which the eventual winner is chosen. More often, this stage is only implicit. But in either case, the prospective client will be assessing proposal candidates in terms of their ability to satisfy both qualification and selection criteria. Maister neatly encapsulates the reason why satisfying the qualification criteria alone is not enough:

> Even the most thorough due diligence . . . usually ends with more than one firm or individual that is qualified to handle [the client's] problem. Most typically, after exhausting my abilities as a client to make technical distinctions, I am still left with a choice of reputable firms with good references, all eminently capable of solving my problem.

> This leads to an important conclusion: unless their skills are truly unique, unmatched by any competitor, professionals are never hired because of their technical abilities. Excellent capabilities are essential to get you into the final set to be considered, but it is other things that get you hired.

Of course, these 'other things' may include a wide range of factors, not least of which is likely to be your proposed fee. But always high on the list is the team's ability to demonstrate that it can develop a strong, mutually rewarding relationship with the client. It is thus that the team must be seen not only as the 'raw material' of your proposal, but also as its salesforce.

It is axiomatic, therefore, that teams should always try to meet the potential client before a final decision is taken, even where this is not a formal requirement of the brief. While this principle is taken for granted in many industries, there are still some sectors – such as the legal profession – where elaborate proposal documents are prepared and submitted without anyone from a participating firm actually going to see the organisation which is conducting the proposal. Without personal contact, the ability for the proposal team to earn the potential client's trust is zero – and without that, the team has only a gambler's chance of succeeding.

Where, however, the team is given ample opportunity to build rapport and trust with the prospective client, another fundamental issue arises: indeed, it is the perennial problem facing those with the responsibility for selecting proposal teams. The team members must satisfy the requirement for technical expertise, or other 'qualification criteria', while at the same time acting as good salesmen, being sensitive to the signals being transmitted by the prospective client and showing empathy and concern. These two sets of attributes, as everyone knows, do not necessarily go together. How then, is it possible to select a team which meets both requirements? In order to assess the possible options, we need to look at the prospective roles of team members on the assignment and in the proposal process.

DEFINING ROLES

One of the underlying themes in successful proposing is ensuring that every member of the team has a clearly defined role: feedback from countless debriefing sessions with client organisations confirms this. Indeed, failure to clarify the roles of the individuals involved seems to create a disproportionately negative impression on decision-makers; what is called into question is not merely how a particular individual will fit into the assignment, but by implication whether the firm has thought through the requirements of the engagement and whether it will be managed effectively. The failure to define team members' roles clearly will also create doubts as to whether the firm has its eye on cost-effectiveness and giving value for money.

The need to define roles applies to the proposal process as well as to the assignment itself. In fact, the proposal leader, together with other senior partners or directors responsible for selecting individuals for an assignment, should start by considering the three separate roles which team members have to play during the course of the proposal. For larger assignments, and to some extent even with small ones, these roles may be divided between different individuals, although there will always be a degree of overlap.

The assignment team role

This will be played by the group of individuals who are to be assigned to the client's business. Some of these individuals, particularly at the more junior level, may not actually meet the client during the course of the proposal process, although the client will generally expect to see a description of their credentials and experience in the proposal document.

The presentation team role

The presentation role describes the individuals which the prospective client sees during the proposal process – including at initial meetings or site visits as well as at the presentation itself. The presentation team will, of course, be a sub-set of the assignment team – tendering organisations generally do not want to see individuals unless it is intended that they will have a role in the assignment.

The proposal team role

The group which performs this function is responsible for managing and expediting the proposal process, and will comprise team members who also have an assignment and presentation role – most notably, the proposal leader. However, proposals can constitute major logistical exercises, and there is often a strong case for using dedicated resources to handle the administrative aspects. For example, someone needs to ensure that appropriate research is commissioned and carried out in the early stages of the process; that deadlines for the production of the proposal document are established and met; that the presentation team is fully briefed on the timetable of the proposal process; that meetings with the prospective client are booked well in advance and find their way into the appropriate diaries; that the presentation rehearsals are arranged and carried out, and so on. It is therefore often advisable to appoint a *proposal manager* to a major tender; his role will be to ensure that the process runs smoothly and that the team's efforts are effectively coordinated, usually without being visible to the prospective client.

The proposal manager will preferably not have a role in the assignment. Delegating the administrative responsibilities in this way also liberates the proposal leader and his colleagues on the presentation team to concentrate on understanding the prospective client's needs and building a strategy for winning the tender.

The proposal manager will also supervise the proposal support function, which may include the design, print and production of the document, and the use of specialist proposal resources – for example, external consultants, presentation coaching specialists and professional writers.

The precise interrelationship between the assignment, presentation and proposal roles will depend on the size and circumstances of the tender, but in many cases can be described graphically as follows:

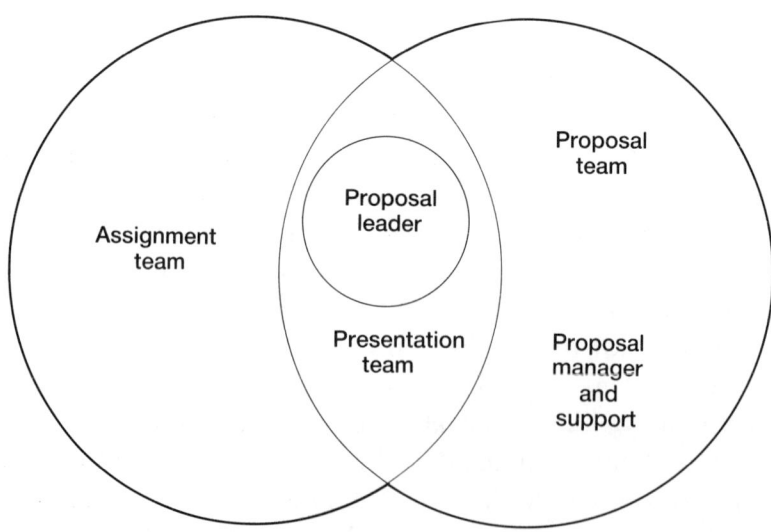

Figure 4.1   Roles

In practice, it will usually be the case that the same individuals are asked to fulfil a number of roles – a member of the assignment team, for example, will also be given responsibility for organising an aspect of the process. The principles that will hold good in nearly all circumstances, however, are that the presentation team should be a sub-set of the assignment team; the proposal leader must combine all three roles, and should be seen to be leading each; and that the proposal manager should not be involved in the assignment or presentation teams.

At the beginning of the proposal process – after having considered whether or not the firm should accept the invitation to tender – one of the proposal leader's first responsibilities is to consider candidates for the assignment, presentation and proposal roles. It may even be a good idea to start filling in names under three columns. This will focus the mind on which individuals should perform which roles. For example, a technically-able specialist who is not thought of as a good communicator may be an essential part of the assignment team; but there may be no necessity for him to be subjected to the rigours of the formal presentation. This will always be a fine balancing act, but there is usually scope to protect poor communicators and promote good ones; provided, that is, the proposal leader himself is perceived to have both the interpersonal skills needed to relate well with the prospective client, and the professional credibility to run the assignment once it's been won.

SELECTING THE ASSIGNMENT TEAM

Deciding who might play a useful role in the proposal process and subsequently on the assignment is, however, only one aspect of team selection. The personal attributes of the individuals who may be nominated for the assignment can't be assessed in isolation: what impression will they make when viewed collectively? And how far do these personal attributes measure up to the role they have been asked to play in the assignment? It is impossible to answer these questions in the abstract: yet experience shows that there are some general principles that shed light on what makes a team convincing and credible.

Proposal leader or professional salesman?

Beware of having a 'professional salesman' on your team. The front man, whose job it is to win the proposal but who will play no significant part in the assignment itself, is regarded with derision by most prospective clients – perhaps because too many of them have been caught out in the past by impressive performance in the presentation followed by non-appearance on the assignment:

> They brought in a front man who we knew would not add to the job. We were therefore not interested in him, it was a waste of time and what he said was irrelevant – we knew he would go away after the tender. We perceived his presence as something to get the contract, and that he'd joined the team to keep us sweet.

Figureheads

A close relative of the professional salesman is the figurehead – a senior partner or director who is drafted onto the team, but for whom no role on the assignment exists. Firms are often seduced into introducing a figurehead because they want to show the extent of their commitment to the prospective client, and that their commitment starts at the top. In practice, however, the figurehead will rarely have participated in the development of the proposal strategy, and may not even understand the key issues facing the target organisation. As a result, the effect is likely to be the opposite of that intended:

> The firm's senior partner rang up and offered to put a very senior colleague on the job. This did not impress us, as we thought he would end up acting out a godfather role and very little else.

The figurehead may also have a detrimental effect on the standing and credibility of the rest of the team:

A very senior partner was fielded late in the process. All that this achieved was to undermine the position of the other partners who'd been involved up until that point.

This, of course, is another instance of the damaging effects of failing to establish clearly defined roles. The introduction of a senior individual who either has no apparent role on the assignment, or whose role is ill-defined, is likely to create uncertainty or apprehension in the mind of the prospective client – and thereafter your prospects of winning the tender will be remote.

Too many chiefs . .

It is usually sensible to nominate one individual who will assume overall responsibility for the assignment. Clients often expect to have a single point of contact with their advisers, and will be confused if offered a choice. Moreover, ambiguity in team leadership will raise doubts about the effectiveness with which the assignment will be managed and directed.

. . . too many Indians

Here it is dangerous to generalise: the optimum distribution of junior and senior resources will depend on the specific requirements of the assignment. However, it is fair to say that clients are often sceptical about the value which junior resources are likely to be able to contribute, and will be suspicious if a significant proportion of the proposed team comprises inexperienced people. In most business areas, organisations are more willing to pay an external adviser for expertise than for manpower. In the words of one finance director:

> In an increasingly risky and complex world, companies want dialogue with experienced staff.

Cost-effectiveness

If organisations do not want their advisers' teams to be over-populated with junior people, then equally they are determined to ensure that where it is appropriate for work to be carried out by lower-level resources, this will be reflected in reduced fees. It is therefore nearly always a mistake to quote a single, composite charging rate for all members of the team. The structure of the team must reflect the proposal leader's analysis of the levels of expertise required to perform the assignment; it is wise to explain this analysis and its fee implications fully to the prospective client.

Balance

Although your firm's chances of succeeding in a tender often depend to a great extent on the proposal leader, it shouldn't be forgotten that in most circumstances the prospective client will be looking for a range of skills, attributes and personalities. The range and balance of the team is therefore a critical factor which needs to be considered before individuals are selected for the proposal.

Acting in concert

It will be helpful if the individuals selected for the team are used to working together, or at least are able to give an impression to that effect. Firms can be remarkably casual about failing to ensure the team members are familiar with each other and each other's methods. For example, the legal director of a major British public company had this to say:

> I was fairly appalled by the way some firms responded [to the tender]. Many just didn't gel as a team. And I interviewed one firm where the two partners put forward to run the assignment had not even met before.

Matching the target's structure

Particularly in assignments which involve complex reporting lines, you should consider proposing a team structure which closely reflects the prospective client's organisation. For example, if it has a matrix structure, in which managers are responsible for, say, both geographical markets and categories of products, you might set up your team to take account of this. Endeavouring to match the prospective client's organisational structure demonstrates flexibility and implies that you have considered how your resources can be deployed most effectively in the light of its specific circumstances and requirements.

Matching culture

This is less tangible, but much more fundamental, than merely endeavouring to match organisational structure. When choosing the team, you need to make an assessment of the style and culture of the organisation which has asked you to propose. Your firm (as represented by the members of the team) must be perceived as being compatible with – preferably sympathetic to – the ethos and values of the prospective client. Even where an organisation is buying services in a sector whose traditions and style are very different from its own (for example, an accountancy firm hiring an advertising agency), the purchaser must still be convinced that he can work effectively with the supplier: indeed all the more so *because* of the cultural divide. So, even if the two organisations are strikingly dissimilar, the proposer must demonstrate that he understands the prospective client's culture and knows how to respond to it.

Even in the earliest stages of the proposal, you should be able to form an impression of the type of culture you're dealing with – or at least an hypothesis which can be subsequently tested through research and site visits. This should influence who from your firm you decide to assign to the team. Cultural factors to watch out for include:

- the scale of the prospective client's ambition. A dynamic, rapidly growing organisation will generally want advisers and suppliers who have an entrepreneurial style and a similar commitment to growth
- whether the organisation is hierarchical or egalitarian. Hierarchical companies will tend to want their advisers to carry out instructions: egalitarian ones will often welcome debate and challenge on how they operate
- whether the organisation is predominantly paternalistic or meritocratic.

Decision-makers will expect their advisers to understand their values, if not share them.

Matching people

Matching prospective team members with what you perceive to be the culture of the target organisation is one thing: but how can you begin to decide whether your people will be personally compatible with the decision makers; whether they will be able to develop a natural rapport? This would seem to be one of the most fundamental issues of all, yet the proposal leader has only his or her intuition to rely on. Sometimes, common sense should provide at least part of the answer, as in the following example:

> We were surprised that one of the firms fielded a team whose members were all not far off retirement. Our directors are all in their early forties, and we pride ourselves on being a company with a fresh, innovative outlook. It was difficult for them to establish a relationship with us because they were not even of the same generation.

It should also be possible to draw some superficial conclusions about the personalities of the decision-makers; whether they are outgoing or introspective, reflective or action-orientated, conformists or individualists and so on. Most proposal leaders, consciously or unconsciously, take these factors into account when considering who should be on the team and who should presented to the prospective client. The real question, however, is whether it is possible to go beyond this: whether, indeed, there might be a more 'scientific' basis for matching your team with the decision-makers on the other side. This is a subject that warrants further discussion.

THE PSYCHOLOGY OF PEOPLE MATCHING

Some business development consultants and presentation specialists maintain that successful people matching can be achieved through the systematic application of psychological principles. While approaches vary, the basic method is as follows.

The underlying concept is that all personality types fall into four broad categories. Every prospective member of the team is given a questionnaire designed to reveal their personality-type. This might involve a list of 40 four-word groups, from which the respondent is asked to choose the word that applies to that individual the most often. The list may be divided between perceived strengths and weaknesses. The adjectives chosen by the respondents are then transferred to a separate sheet which regroups them according to four personality descriptors: 'analyser', 'driver', 'amiable' and 'expressive'. Each descriptor has a range of personality traits associated with it. For example, analysers tend to be thoughtful and unassuming, prefer reflection to action and are task rather than people-oriented. Expressives tend to be the opposite: they are outgoing and friendly, inclined to generalise and exaggerate and are natural salesmen. Drivers are usually ambitious, self-confident and strong willed, but tend to hide their feelings. Amiables are sensitive, eager to please, patient. They are more likely to solicit the opinions of others than to try to impose their own. Respondents who choose most words belonging to the 'analysers' category must then learn to think of themselves as 'analysers', and so on. To this primary descriptor can be added a qualifying descriptor corresponding to the category in which the second largest number of adjectives was chosen, making for 16 possible combinations.

How is this type of personality profiling relevant to selecting the team for a proposal? The theory is that your chances of success will be considerably enhanced if you can match the personality types of your team with those of the prospective client. The assumptions upon which this claim is based would seem to be:

- the personality of the service provider is one of the most critical factors in influencing the prospective client's decision
- people have a natural tendency to buy from individuals who they perceive to be like themselves
- the methodology described is an effective means of categorising personality
- it is possible to make an accurate prima facie assessment of the personality types of the decision-makers.

While the theory is intriguing, none of these assumptions should go unchallenged. Personality is important in a proposal, because the prospective client will tend to favour individuals or teams which he or she wants to work with. But this is more likely to be an eliminator rather than a success factor. If it is obvious at your first meeting with a new business contact that your prospective relationship is likely to be riven with discord, it won't surprise you if the contract is eventually awarded to someone else. But it would be wrong to assume that an apparently friendly initial meeting will have the opposite effect. Most prospective clients will be courteous and friendly with each of the firms they have asked to propose; and it is only at the presentation, when the final decision is looming, that they are likely to become more adversarial. Even if you get on like a house on fire, it is always a mistake to assume that this alone will enable you to succeed. Prospective clients will usually endeavour to be as objective as possible throughout the process, and will be on their guard against forming a favourable view of a contender purely because everyone seemed to get on well. Indeed, one of the most fundamental errors committed by proposal teams is to assume that just because they've had cordial meetings with the prospective client, the assignment is as good as in the bag.

Do people buy from people they believe are like themselves? To some extent, perhaps. But sometimes the opposite is the case. For example, an advertising agency (expressives galore) may well be looking for a set of personal characteristics, as well as skills, which are quite different from their own when they consider hiring an accountancy firm (analysers to a man). Such as prudence, discipline, attention to detail – and maybe not too much flair. Or picture a particularly timid and introspective businessman involved in a major piece of litigation – might he not prefer to have a spectacularly aggressive litigator representing his interests? Of course, it can be argued that the personality profiling method could be used to select a team whose members are conspicuously different in character from the decision-makers; but then how do you know when to choose the team which is different, or similar, in this respect?

Is the methodology effective? Certainly, there is much about this way of categorising personality which rings true. One possible flaw is that the self-assessment questionnaire has no means of distinguishing between how respondents see themselves and how, perhaps, they would prefer to be seen. There may be, therefore, an aspirational aspect to the adjectives respondents select to describe themselves.

The greatest difficulty, however, lies in how the method can be practically applied in proposal situations. As you are unlikely to feel very comfortable about asking the prospective client to submit to a formal personality test, the best you can do is to guess which category he or she belongs to. This itself may be of value, but must undermine the method's scientific pretensions.

In summary, personality profiling is an interesting academic exercise and one which may be genuinely useful in providing some structure to the way you assess the personal characteristics of your team members and their opposite numbers from the target organisation. But it would be erroneous to assume that such a method will guarantee that you will win more than your fair share of proposals. Of course, it is important to be sensitive to the prospective client's personal characteristics, as well as his ideas and attitudes. But second-guessing them is dangerous. Clients usually want advisers who have their own ideas and approaches, not ones who try to work out what the clients are thinking in order to tell them what they want to hear. Similarly, basing your strategy on choosing a team which will fit in with what you perceive to be the personal characteristics of the decision-makers is too passive an approach to succeed very often. Having the confidence and authority to say what you really think – and to be yourself – is a much surer way to get results.

KEY POINTS

- Every effort should be made to meet the prospective client before the final decision is taken; without personal contact, your chances of success will be minimal.

- In large or complex tenders, appoint a manager from outside the team to handle the day-to-day logistics.

- Every member of the team must have a clearly defined role; failure to clarify roles will lead the prospective client to question your management skills.

- Those attending the oral presentation should be drawn from the assignment team.

- Introducing a 'professional salesman' into your team – especially half-way through the proposal – is likely to create uncertainty and apprehension within the target organisation.

- Nominate only one individual to lead your proposal, and be careful not to pack your team with too many junior staff; the balance of senior and lower-level resources must be appropriate to the potential client's commercial objectives and budgetary constraints.

- Wherever possible, try to ensure that your team is used to working together and that its structure matches that of the target organisation.

- Assess the style and culture of the organisation to which you are proposing, and how well the team fits in.

- Do not take 'people-matching' too far; remember that most clients want advisers with their own ideas and approaches rather than individuals who will tell them only what they think the client wants to hear.

5

RESEARCH METHODS

THE NEED FOR QUALITY

The critical success factors matrix will have set the broad direction in which you should be pursuing your research. Now you need to explore all the available avenues.

This will very much depend on the nature of the organisation to which are proposing. It is, of course, far easier to acquire data on and opinions about a large listed company than a small owner-managed business. This doesn't mean, however, that quantity equals quality: it could be that a chance remark about the managing director's inability to concentrate on a document for more than ten minutes will be far more useful to you than a decades' worth of annual reports and accounts. This is no excuse, however, for not trying to find out as much as you can about the prospective client.

The many sources of information open to you can essentially be grouped together into two broad categories: desk research and personal contacts.

DESK RESEARCH

Desk research is essentially anything that has been written down or stored in a computer about – and by – the target organisation which is publicly available (and in a few cases, perhaps, which is not publicly available). There is a large variety of information you can trawl.

Financial data

If your target is quoted on a major stock exchange, acquiring the accounts is straightforward – if the corporation is British, telephone the company secretary's department. Where it is a limited company (again in the UK), you can obtain copies of the filed accounts from Companies House. There are also any number of databases from which you can extract the relevant figures about financial performance, in addition to press coverage and (where the company is listed) stockbrokers' circulars.

There is no need to become bogged down in the figures – not least because they will often be a year or more out of date and, indeed, may have had certain creative accounting techniques applied to them. Depending on the territory in which your target files its accounts – the US is probably the most comprehensive in terms of financial disclosure – you should normally be able to form a reasonable picture of which areas of the business are growing, and which are not.

More helpful in many cases is the chairman's and directors' reports which usually accompany the figures. While you will not find any trade secrets, they will often give you a good idea of where the management sees the company's future, and which segments of the business are likely to be the main focus of attention.

Internal literature

No-one is suggesting that you should break into the organisation's offices in the dead of night and rifle the files for secret memoranda. But it is often easy, and perfectly legal, to acquire copies of internal corporate literature. These can tell you a great deal about culture, personalities and, sometimes, approach to decision-making.

Staff newsletters are a good example. Sanitised as they usually are (there will be no accounts of the latest boardroom ruction), scanning some back issues can shed considerable light on the organisation. For instance, that it has a newsletter at all suggests that management has more than a passing interest in the motivation and welfare of its employees. What kind of messages are they attempting to convey: is the tone smug and self-satisfied, or is the company genuinely trying to engender a team spirit?

Look at the 'promotions' and 'new people' columns: who have they worked for previously, and what new areas of business have been established to warrant the changed responsibilities? Staff newsletters will often provide a short cut to forming a clearer idea of individual areas of responsibility: your contact may have been promoted to head of purchasing, or be mentioned in the context of a piece about new contracts which shows that he specialises in project development work. Newsletters are likely to provide you with far higher quality information than telephone conversations with switchboard operators.

The same pieces about management changes might also give you an idea of decision-making procedures. If closer reading suggests that your contact's promotion to head of purchasing actually means he is joining the 15-strong north eastern purchasing committee, you may have to think again about whether he can exercise much influence on your behalf.

Do not believe everything you read, but consider the overall tone being set by these publications and read between the lines. Approached in this way, newsletters can give you a surprisingly good feel for the prospective client.

Product and service literature

Obtain copies of the potential client's brochures and service leaflets. They will not provide you with a comprehensive list of everything the organisation does, but they are likely to give an indication of the areas on which the company is concentrating effort and, conversely, which areas need support. The various contact names may also help you decide where internal responsibilities lie.

Consider, too, how this material *looks*. If it is lavish and expensive, your written submission should probably have a similar feel. If it is basic and workmanlike, it may be that the decision-makers will consider a glossy proposal document to be rather excessive.

Other publicity and recruitment material

The same principles apply to the company's other promotional material. For example, what kind of impression is conveyed by its advertising? Which services or products do the campaigns promote? What does this tell you about marketing strengths and objectives?

Recruitment advertisements are even more important. Scan the relevant trade and national press to see whether the target is looking for additional personnel. Are the ads for new or existing positions? What does the job description suggest about the organisation's activities and future intentions? It may be, for example, that the company needs new people in a specific area. Part of your proposal, therefore, might include the offer to provide contracted-out resources for performing these functions at a competitive rate.

Market information

Every proposal demands that you form an understanding of the trading conditions and competitive forces which characterise the prospective client's marketplace. Even when you have your own in-house experts, find out what you can from other information sources; certainly, the team leader should not rely solely on second-hand knowledge if he wishes to feel comfortable with the subject.

Look through some of the key trade journals to enhance your knowledge of the main issues currently affecting the industry. This should also help you form a picture of what the prospective client's competitors are doing.

You can acquire any number of reports and statistics about market share, trends and developments in a particular sector. Quantitative and qualitative research is available from research companies, data processors, newspapers, professional firms and so on. In the UK, these include:

- financial information: Financial Times Business Information (FTBI), McCarthy's, Reuters, Extel
- market research/information: Mintel, Economist Intelligence Unit, Keynote
- press coverage: Textline, FTBI.

Given the price tag often attached to the surveys and other forms of market information, however, make sure that the data is relevant to your enquiries and provides sufficient detail for you to draw sensible conclusions. Being told that your target is ranked first in the sector when there is no information about who is second or third will not help you very much.

At the very beginning of the research phase, draw up a checklist like the one in Fig. 5.1. Starting with the left-hand column, write down every 'public' information source you can conceivably think of under a series of general headings. Then decide how relevant each source is to your enquiries and the extent to which it is likely to prove useful. Allocate responsibilities among your team for retrieving the data, and use the last column on the right-hand side to make a note of when that particular avenue of research has been covered to your satisfaction.

USING CONTACTS

The information of most use to you is the sort which comes from people, rather than books, brochures or computers. But think about what you want to ask them first; journalists, for example, give short shrift to public relations consultants who 'phone up and say, 'We're doing a pitch to Acme Products – do you know anything about them?'. You cannot expect someone else to do your research for you.

You do not have to wait until all your desk research is finished, but you should make sure that you know the basics about the

Information Source	Critical	Useful	Marginal value	Not relevant/ applicable	Date completed
Financial Report & accounts Interim reports Companies House/ published accounts FTBI Hambros					
Services/products Product literature Directory entries Advertisements					
Market share Marketing databases Keynote reports					
Competitors Market research Press coverage					
Culture Corporate briefings Internal newsletters					
Recent history Press coverage Annual reviews					
Future intentions Recruitment advertising Brokers' circulars					
Future market *developments* Press coverage EIU and other reports					

Figure 5.1   Desk research checklist

organisation before you start your enquiries. If not, you will squander goodwill and waste the opportunity to find out something which probably will be unavailable through other sources. After all, you want opinions and, where possible, inside knowledge from these individuals; the facts and figures should be retrieved from a library.

Who can help you?

Your colleagues

The people with whom you work are probably the best place to start. They may know things about the prospective client or its industry sector which you do not; they may also know some of the individuals within the organisation – perhaps because they have worked with them in other jobs, or have friends and relations who are employed there. In addition, they might be able to effect introductions to professional advisers and others who will know something about the potential client.

It may also be that your colleagues have sold products or services to the organisation in the past. You should always double-check this: it is important to know whether your firm has had any previous contact, and the form which this contact took. Who did your colleagues deal with? Were there any problems which damaged the relationship? If so, are the same people in charge, and are they likely to hold their previous experience of your firm against you?

Obvious as it may seem, make sure that yours is the only unit or group within your organisation which is proposing for the business. There have been occasions when different territories in large international groups have submitted entirely separate proposals in response to the same brief. Few things could be more inept.

Your clients

There is nothing wrong with asking existing clients about an organisation you are proposing to (unless they are direct competitors). It would be foolish not to explore their knowledge of companies which operate in a similar area of business.

Clients will often feel flattered that you have sought their opinion. Those that you have worked with for a long time may like the idea of helping your business in this way; the majority of people will be only too happy to help. But make sure that you get a view from your clients' junior people as well as those at senior management levels.

The sales force, for instance, can probably tell you a good deal about the organisation's ability to deliver on time and within budget. The accounts department, on the other hand, might be able to give you a steer on payment times or even cashflow. If that seems unlikely, remember that most people involved in a particular business know another person who does the same job somewhere else; they meet each other at conferences and seminars, and will often talk quite candidly about their own organisations.

Taking advantage of this potentially vast bank of knowledge costs you nothing. Moreover, by asking you may help to strengthen your relationship with existing clients.

Professional advisers

Don't forget contacts you may have with the organisation's existing advisers – their lawyers, auditors, bankers, insurance brokers and so on. You do not have to ask them to be betray any confidences, but there is no reason why they cannot discuss with you the personalities of those who take the decisions, and what they tend to expect of their advisers. How efficiently and quickly, for example, do directors respond to requests for information? Are they prepared to be guided by their advisers in difficult situations, or do they simply like to issue instructions which they prefer not to be questioned? The answers could be important in deciding how you approach the proposal, and the kind of people your team should include.

Think about the organisation's advisers in the broadest possible terms. The CEO, for instance, might place considerably more weight on the opinions of his private media relations 'guru' than his investment banker; as a result, the former may be able to give you a far better idea of what he intends to do with the company over the long term.

Market commentators

Where you can draw on an acquaintanceship or contact, probe the opinions of those whose job it is to know about the target and its markets, such as analysts and journalists. Ask these people what they think of the quality of management and how it tackles problems; find out how they think the organisation compares with its competitors; and ask them to give a view on the company's future. Again, you will find that many people who follow a sector or industry for professional reasons are only too pleased to help you informally (provided you have done your homework first).

You might even go one step further and draft an industry analyst or other external specialist onto your team, either to advise behind the scenes on the proposal or, in exceptional circumstances, to act as a consultant on the assignment team itself. In these situations, of course, you will need to pay a fee; but the former initiative may help you to develop some fresh insight into the prospective client's business and objectives, while the latter could demonstrate that you have understood which skills are required to undertake the assignment effectively and are prepared to reach outside your own firm to put together the right combination of expertise. Both options are clearly worth considering.

Personal contacts

Last but by no means least, consider what you may be able to find out from your other personal contacts. These may include:

- non-executive directors: if you know someone who is – or has been – on the company's board in a non-executive capacity, ask them about the key decision-makers. Who are they, what are their areas of responsibility and what qualities do they look for in their advisers? How are board meetings managed in practice? For instance, are they lengthy, democratic affairs where everyone is encouraged to have their say, or does the chairman or CEO simply seek a rubber stamp for his decisions from his fellow directors?

- ex-employees: non-executive or otherwise, ask for the opinions of people who have worked for the organisation in the past. How do they rate their former colleagues; what are their personal strengths and weaknesses, and what are they like to work with?
- trade associations: consider whether any trade bodies to which the organisation belongs can give you a steer on the decision-makers. Are they active participants and do they lobby hard on key industry issues? If so, which issues do they tend to campaign on?
- trades unionists: it may be that you have links with the organisation's workforce through its shopfloor representatives. What is their view of the prevailing management style? Is it paternalistic, combative or merely indifferent? How good is management's relationship with the workforce, and where are the key areas of contention?

Before you start probing your colleagues and contacts, draw up a similar checklist (Fig. 5.2) to the one you produced for your desk research. List all the types of people whose opinions you think would be helpful and, as before, gauge their likely value as a source of information.

Whoever you speak to, try to make the most of each opportunity by testing initial opinions or hypotheses. Rather than devote the entire conversation to open-ended questions, ask your contact to comment on the views of others or on a specific line of approach which you may be considering for the proposal itself. This will enable you to test some initial ideas, and help you to decide whether they are worth raising with the potential client during the interview stage.

Information Source	Critical	Useful	Marginal value	Not relevant/ applicable	Date completed
Colleagues					
Ex-employees					
Bankers					
Stockbrokers					
Financial journalists					
Investor relations advisers					
Auditors					
Lawyers					
Insurance brokers					
PR consultants/ lobbyists					
Legislators					
Trade journalists					
Trade associations					

Figure 5.2   Contacts research checklist

USING WHAT YOU HAVE DISCOVERED

You can often go on forever in the research phase. There is always some other piece of material to read, or one more person to speak to. Obviously, the limited timescale within which most tenders are conducted will act as a natural constraint, but be careful not to get carried away with the task.

Above all, be selective. Not only are you faced by time constraints; you will also find that much of what you discover is not relevant to the development of your case. If you have gone to considerable lengths in your research, the risk is that you will be tempted to use all of the information in the document or presentation in order to show how hard you have worked.

If that happens, the chances are that you will simply be telling the decision-makers what they already know. Research will help you understand the organisation and its market, but its primary purpose is to discover an issue or an 'angle' from which you can create a compelling proposition – it is *not* to tell the prospective client about his or her own business. The decision-makers know about the company's products, financial performance and competitors. You need to demonstrate that you understand the significance of these things, too, but regurgitating facts and figures is not the way to demonstrate that knowledge.

The second risk at the end of an in-depth research exercise is that none of the material is actually used. Everyone feels better for having done it, but no-one has the time or inclination to think about how it should be incorporated into the proposal. The team reverts to some tired old boilerplate, and sends in the usual credentials document after the names have been changed on the word-processor.

This happens alarmingly often. It is not uncommon, for instance, to find proposal teams which will commission management consultants (usually at great cost) to undertake an exhaustive survey of the potential client's industry and position within the marketplace. A large report arrives on the team leader's desk three weeks later, which is subsequently handed to a junior who is told to 'see if you can find anything useful in this'. This is usually impossible, and the net result is wasted time, effort and money.

It is the team leader's job to control and direct the research, and then to interpret it. Maintain a clear focus on why you are doing the research, and make sure you use and extrapolate from your findings. Otherwise it cannot work for you.

KEY POINTS

- Use the critical success factors matrix for directing the overall thrust of your investigations, and draw up separate checklists for assessing the relative importance of information likely to be derived from public sources and personal contacts.

- Exploit every possible source of publicly available information on the target organisation, including financial data, product and service literature, publicity and recruitment material, press coverage and other analyses produced by market commentators.

- Where you can, try to acquire copies of the organisation's internal newsletters; they can be invaluable in helping you assess important corporate developments, and management culture and objectives.

- Look for key issues and themes which emerge from written material produced by or about the potential client; these will provide you with a clearer understanding of the context in which the tender has arisen and any additional needs not covered by the brief.

- The highest quality information will be derived from personal contacts; ask your colleagues, clients, advisers and specialists who follow the market what they know about the prospective client's needs, objectives and decision-makers.

- Don't forget current or past employees of the organisation; they will be particularly useful in forming an assessment of management style and culture, and attitudes towards advisers.

- Where appropriate, consider drafting in an external analyst or specialist consultant to ensure that your team has access to in-depth market information and technical expertise.

- Use interviews to compare differing analyses and opinions, and to gauge reaction to your initial hypotheses and ideas.

- Regard your discussions with personal contacts as opportunities to acquire opinions and inside information; don't squander them by asking for facts or figures.

- The team leader must direct and control the team's research to ensure that it is effectively collated, analysed and interpreted and, above all, that the key findings are used to enhance your proposal; there is no point to research which simply tells the decision-makers what they already know.

6

INTERVIEWS

WHY SITE VISITS MATTER

The importance of the interview stage cannot be overestimated. A poor performance in site visits can very quickly knock your firm out of the running, while a strong showing could put you way ahead of the rest of the field.

Why do site visits matter so much? Put yourself in the position of the prospective client, and imagine you had asked three different advisers to propose for your business.

Adviser One fails to arrange any interviews before submitting his document, even though you have made it absolutely clear that you are willing to talk about your requirements with him in person at any time. He might be an extremely competent and likeable man but, because you did not have an opportunity to meet him, you will never know.

Adviser Two takes up your offer, but sends a team of five to what seems like an interminable series of meetings – always with you. The four team members who do not say anything are more than compensated for by the fifth, who spends 95 per cent of the time telling you how marvellous his organisation is. When he does ask you questions, you realise that you are talking about subjects which are either irrelevant to what you want him to do or have already been fully explained in your written invitation to tender.

Adviser Three arranges three one-hour meetings immediately after he has received your brief: one with you, another with the finance director and a third with your senior production manager. You do not see all of his team because they have split up to handle each of these meetings, but the reports you get back are favourable. Everyone on their team listens to what your people have to say, they make initial suggestions about niggling problems which you have been worried about, and they clearly know what is happening in your industry.

Your session with the team leader goes particularly well. He does not say very much about his firm's resources and experience; instead, he talks about what your competitors are doing, how market demand is changing and suggests a stance you might take on a proposed piece of legislation. He also asks you a variety of questions about how the business has developed, where the pressure points are, how the new product line is coming along and so on.

You cannot help liking him, but not because it turns out that he reads the same fiction as you or sends his children to the same school as yours. What makes you like him is his interest in what you are trying to achieve; his familiarity with the issues you have to tackle every day; the way it is obvious he has addressed very identical problems in similar companies; and how he seems capable of getting the best out of the people he manages.

Which of the three would impress *you*?

STRIKING THE RIGHT BALANCE

Don't go overboard if the prospective client has indicated that you can conduct as many interviews as you feel like. Open is not the same as unlimited access, so be careful about the number of visits you ask for. You want to avoid this kind of reaction:

> From the moment they got the invitation to tender, they were constantly turning up at the offices, telephoning our people and generally pressurising us.

You do not need to crawl over an organisation to gain advantage. On the contrary, be selective about your requests for meetings, and think carefully about whom you should approach.

Who will be expecting to see you and, conversely, who will not? Which people are going to provide you with the best steer on the organisation's needs and culture? Who is likely to be able to tell you things which will give you an inside track, and whose knowledge is limited?

Be careful not to waste time with people who do not have the right information or may lead you down a blind alley. That is easier said than done, but consider what their roles in the organisation tell you about their knowledge or influence. For instance, the internal audit manager may be extremely helpful to you in assessing how effectively the organisation manages its cashflow, but is unlikely to be able to give you any insight into long-term funding arrangements. Remember that your judgement may be called into question if the decision-makers believe that you have spent time with people who do not understand what the organisation is attempting to achieve through the tender.

A selective approach is also important for reasons of time and cost. If the team leader is too busy attending meetings with the potential client, he or she may lose sight of the overall picture and get bogged down in detail. And, obviously, you could find yourself paying heavily in both direct and opportunity costs if you take up every suggestion offered in a meeting, especially where international proposals are concerned. It is the team leader's responsibility to manage the schedule and costs of site visits effectively, and to make sure that they do not assume a life of their own.

What should you do when the potential client has not said anything about interviews? There are a number of instances where no site visits take place at all, either because of tight timescales or because the pre-proposal 'courting' of the organisation makes them largely unnecessary. In the latter case, the tender may represent the formal culmination of a very long period of intelligence-gathering, or persuasion of the potential client to undertake a specific project. Going over all the same ground again would be counter-productive; you will already have acquired a sound idea of what the organisation needs.

All the same, make sure you talk to the potential client about the logistics of the proposal and who will be taking the final decision. You may have convinced your particular contact to embark on the project, but what does he need to see from you in order to gain the support of his colleagues and persuade them that yours is the best firm for the job? How many other organisations have been asked to tender, and why were they selected? How much do the other decision-makers know about your approach, and how can you fill in the gaps in their knowledge? What kind of messages will they be looking for in your document and at the presentation? However much spadework you have done in the run-up to the tender, the goalposts will have moved a little by the time the proposal enters its formal stages. Find out how.

Even where the buyer has specified that there will be no interviews, you should at least have a telephone conversation with the individual responsible for managing the tender within the organisation. Better still if you can convince him to change his mind. There are certain to be a number of issues within the brief which you feel need to be clarified – or which provide a pretext for having a meeting. Although they may wish to appear remote at first, many people will agree to a meeting if you make it clear that you want to talk about the proposed assignment, not yourself.

The worst of both worlds, of course, is to be offered the opportunity of interviewing the potential client and then fail to do anything about it. The impression created is always unfavourable:

> We were surprised by how few of the tendering firms came to talk to us before submitting their proposal. We were more than happy to give them the time, but hardly any bothered to take it. Inevitably, these firms didn't figure in our final decision.

What would your reaction be if you had asked someone to paint your house and they submitted an estimate without ever having seen it? The principle applies with equal force to corporate tenders. Moreover, you do not need to see whether you can get on with the man who paints your house before you give him the job. But if you are a board director who will have to establish a productive working relationship with a prospective set of bankers, you will certainly wish to assess their qualities as individuals before appointing them.

CLARIFYING THE BRIEF

As we mentioned earlier, what clients say they want is seldom all that they need. However comprehensive the written brief, you must use the site visits to clarify their requirements.

Is it a test?

It is not simply that clients don't always know what they want. Many deliberately provide only the most basic of tender invitations in order to test the skills of competing firms in identifying their needs. Invidious as this may seem, it is a perfectly legitimate way for buyers to approach a proposal situation.

The test can take one (or more) of several forms. The target may give you an unusually short period in which to research and submit your proposal. You may also find that they say nothing about site visits in their brief. This seldom means that they won't give you the time; it can instead be a device to see which firms take the initiative and ask for an interview.

The converse also applies. The prospective client will propose a punishing schedule of site visits, either to determine whether you are capable of marshalling sufficient resources to carry them all out, or whether you are prepared to challenge their purpose. If you do not think you need to undertake every visit they suggest, tactfully say so and give your reasons – for instance, because you believe that the activities of Subsidiary One are more relevant to the approach you are likely to recommend than those of Subsidiary Two.

Whether the brief looks like a test or has simply been drafted badly, serious potential clients will be looking for concrete signs that you can successfully anticipate their needs:

The winning firm offered us a different kind of package which would provide what we wanted. But since we didn't really know what we wanted, we expected each of the firms to tell us what we needed. They understood this perfectly, and won the job.

Site visits are a critical part of defining what will benefit the potential client most. There may, for instance, be some strange inclusions in the invitation to tender which you feel are either irrelevant or unrealistic. Tactfully ask the organisation why these requirements have been specified, and point out what the difficulties would be in meeting them – for example, ineffective use of their management time, or extra cost. The brief may not have been put together very carefully; if it is excessively long or repetitious, go through it with the potential client and find out what the organisation is really looking for.

Filling in the gaps

On the other hand, you may feel that the brief fails to address a number of important areas. Use your site visits to establish what the key people need you to do on a point-by-point basis; if the conversation suggests that they don't know, propose some requirements yourself and see what their reaction is.

As we know, helping the potential client to clarify the brief can pay significant dividends – even to the extent of aborting the tender process. While this is unlikely in most cases, making sure that the target has comprehensively covered all the requisite areas can only do you good. It shows your ability to think laterally about the prospective client's circumstances and, by not taking everything at face value, suggests yours is the type of organisation which is likely to make a strong contribution.

Be careful, though, that you are not perceived to be tearing the brief apart because you want to provide an entirely different service to the one you've been asked to propose for – or because a widening of the brief will enable you to generate considerably more revenue from the assignment. The clarification of the brief should be a constructive process, designed to identify the potential client's needs with greater precision.

LOGISTICS

As with every other area of proposal activity, the conduct of site visits raises a number of logistical and administrative issues.

Agendas

Where major site visits are involved, send an agenda in advance. In addition to making clear to the potential client what you want from them, this will create a favourable impression of your ability to think ahead and to use their time effectively. Take the trouble to draw up separate agendas for each meeting, too; a 'standard' list of questions or issues which could apply to any organisation of a similar size or type will strike the interviewer as careless and irrelevant.

If you feel it is appropriate, write him a note of thanks when you get back to the office. Do not, however, say anything about how your proposal is developing at this stage; it may be that you will need to change tack completely in the light of your later findings. Avoid creating any hostages to fortune.

Scheduling your site visits

If you have to undertake a large number of site visits across a variety of locations, think about the timing. There is little point in conducting interviews after you have submitted your document or before brainstorming the invitation to tender. As we said in Chapter 5, site visits are critical to understanding what preoccupies and motivates the decision-makers; using them as vehicles for data-gathering or other forms of basic research will irritate the prospective client and squander a key opportunity to create competitive advantage.

Leave yourself enough time to consider what you have learned from the site visits. Although it is not always possible, try to avoid having to send the document the day after your interview with the chairman. Not only are you unlikely to have time to incorporate your findings, you will also be unable to verify or compare anything he might have told you against information from other sources.

Absorbing the key messages

The key messages which emerge from every interview need to be written down in a post-meeting memorandum, distributed among and discussed by the whole proposal team. Be suspicious of any of your colleagues who claim that they would prefer to brief you orally. It may mean that their line of questioning was inappropriate, antagonistic or irrelevant. If all know in advance of the site visits that they will be obliged to make a note of their discussions afterwards, they are much more likely to come back with some real information.

My place or yours?

Consider where the interviews should take place. Always aim to hold your meeting at the potential client's premises. This will give you an opportunity to see their people at work in their own context, to meet their colleagues, and to form an impression of the characteristics of the organisation. However communicative and helpful an individual might appear to be away from the office, you will never be able to form the same rounded opinion if he or she is sitting the other side of your own desk.

Try to avoid interviews over lunch or dinner – at least in the first instance. Leaving aside the obvious effects of alcohol, you may find that your contact is unwilling to discuss difficult issues in a public restaurant or bar, or that he gets too easily distracted in a social setting. Proposers inclined to regard the site visit phase as little more than a series of agreeable lunchtime excursions should stay in the office and save themselves the money.

Later on in the proposal process you may decide that the key individuals are more likely to give you an inside track over a drink or dinner. But be careful about issuing invitations of this sort; they might be misinterpreted as unbusiness-like, outright bribery, or simply a waste of time.

Additional meetings

If there is a great deal to discuss and you run out of time, you may want to propose additional meetings. You should be cautious, however, about requesting further site visits – there are limits to a prospective client's time and, of course, patience. Successful site visits are not a question of spending as many hours with the potential client as you possibly can; they are about making best use of the time which you have been given. Go back if you are specifically asked to, or if it transpires that there is a key part of the operations which the interviewee has forgotten to tell you about previously.

Generally speaking, however, the invitation to tender and your pre-interview research should have given you a good idea of how extensive your site visits should be. Certainly, never ask to go back because you have failed to understand what you've been told the first time around. The time to clarify the information you have been sent is during the interviews themselves – not several days later.

DEPLOYING THE TEAM

The interview stage usually offers the potential client his or her first full opportunity to meet you and your team. You have to ensure, therefore, that the people you put forward are carefully selected and, of course, that they interview the right individuals. A significant lapse in judgement during this key phase can easily kill your chances stone dead.

Who should go?

In some cases, the potential client will specify whom he wishes to see from your organisation. This would typically include, for instance, the individual in overall charge of the assignment and the person responsible for managing the job on a day-to-day basis. In a majority of tenders, however, the choice is likely to be left up to you.

Do not make the mistake of thinking that the proposal leader is the only person who should conduct site visits – or, for that matter, who should act as the 'front' for all such meetings. On large assignments where the potential client requires and is looking for signs of your ability to field teams at several different levels, it will not be necessary for you to lead every interview. If you are sure of your team's competence and skills, there should be no reason for you to feel reluctant about putting them forward.

The best policy is to match your team with that of the potential client's and allocate the interviews according to the reporting lines which will exist if you win the job. That way, everyone will get to meet their opposite numbers and to begin forming an idea of what they will be like to work with. Inevitably, there will be exceptions. You as proposal leader may need to speak to someone comparatively junior in the organisation in order to form a clearer picture of a particular important activity or business unit. Furthermore, it may be that a senior potential buyer of your services wants to meet all your people – however peripheral they may be to the assignment – to feel reassured that they are suitable (or, indeed, that they actually exist).

Exercise judgement and discretion. In an interview with the CEO about the company's long-term financial strategy, there is no point in taking along the trainee who will provide day-to-day support for your managers. The CEO will have serious doubts about your ability to understand where your firm's resources need to be focused; he or she is also unlikely, of course, to want to discuss sensitive issues in front of a callow apprentice.

Who should we interview?

The initial brief and your critical path should have given you a clear idea of whom you need to spend time with at the organisation. But discuss the issue with your primary contact: tell him who you think you need to see and why, and ask for suggestions. Most people will be more than happy to direct you to the right people.

The individuals you should interview generally fall into two camps: those who have the detailed knowledge you need in order to develop a comprehensive response to the brief; and those whose responsibilities and/or influence will be critical to the outcome. Some people, of course, will have a foot in both camps – the directors of owner-managed businesses frequently fall into this category.

It is easy enough to request time with the first group. The second, however, may be more problematic. As with all proposals activity, everything you do needs to have a reason. Don't ask for an interview with the chairman simply because 'we think it would be a good idea'. Tell him (or your contact) that you feel you need to meet because there are a number of issues which require his contribution. Even if this is not strictly true, contrive a sound pretext for getting together and still make sure you have something sensible and relevant to ask him.

Do this only if the chairman is likely to be one of the key decision-makers or influencers, however. Don't ask for interviews with individuals who are not relevant to the proposal or decision-making function because you believe this will curry favour in some way. No-one likes to have their time wasted, and going straight to the top for no obvious reason is sure to alienate both those you interview and the people who have been put in charge of the tender decision.

How many should we take?

Do not pile in with your entire team for every interview. This will appear intimidating and raise serious doubts about your managerial skills:

One firm turned up with no fewer than six people for one meeting with me. It was completely over the top for what was only an initial fact-finding session.

Six-to-one is a ridiculous ratio in any set of circumstances; however good your people are, they will never be able to demonstrate their qualities in a forum of this size. It is far better to be outnumbered by the potential client than the other way around. The basic rule is: don't exceed their numbers with your own.

What are you doing here?

Above all, make sure that anyone who goes on a site visit has a clearly defined role in the discussions and, moreover, is seen by the potential client to have a good reason for being there. That reason will nearly always be because he or she has a role in the assignment itself.

Explain how each individual present fits into the team. Clarify what their roles will be, and give them some questions to ask and issues to discuss. There is no such thing as safety in numbers:

> There were always at least two people in the meetings who didn't say anything. We just couldn't help wondering what on earth they'd be doing if the firm had been given the job.

Nothing is worse than turning up with four people, of which only one does the talking. The prospective client will be forced to ask himself whether, if you are given the work, the silent majority is going to have anything to contribute and, worse still, whether they will be on the assignment solely to inflate the fees.

THE RIGHT APPROACH

Be thorough in your pre-interview planning, and think hard about how you can get the best results from these critical meetings.

Structuring the discussion

Even when you are not sending an agenda in advance, you must have a clear idea before you start talking of the areas you need to cover. Don't be too rigid about your agenda, however. The secret of a successful site visit lies in your ability to focus the discussion on the key issues, and to direct it away from those which will not lead anywhere. You will not necessarily know what these issues are until the discussion begins, so you must be prepared to think on your feet and change tack whenever necessary. Don't worry about departing from the formal agenda if you hit a particularly rich seam; the potential client won't mind and, since you are unlikely to have the same chance again, you must use the opportunity to the full. It will quickly become apparent what is and is not important.

Are we going too far?

Think very carefully about what and how much you need to know from the people you interview. Many proposers fall into the trap of thinking that the best way to create a good impression in site visits is to ignore anything that looks like detail and concentrate on the macro issues.

Obviously, it depends on what you are being asked to tender for. But you must keep your questioning relevant. If you are proposing for the audit of a comparatively small subsidiary, for example, you do not need to know everything about the company's five-year strategic plan:

> We were puzzled and irritated by what struck us as far too much delving into our corporate strategy – it simply wasn't material to what we were asking them to do.

Even where the big issues are relevant, you may find yourself having to approach them very circuitously. The potential client may only have just met you; he is unlikely, therefore, to divulge his company's innermost secrets to a group of people who are more or less strangers. Moreover, part of what the company is looking for may well be your skills in identifying what these issues are without having to spell them out at the first meeting. Others may simply regard your line of questioning as impertinent.

Handling the questioning

On many issues, you won't be able to be as direct with your questioning as you would like. Striding up to the finance director and saying 'Is it true that your loss of the Acme Products contract will wipe out all of next year's profits?' is unlikely to be very well received. Even if it is true, it would be better to ask, 'What effect do you think the loss of the Acme contract will have on next year's profitability?'.

By all means test your hypotheses and information from other sources, but be tactful. Remember that you are not an investigative journalist; you have to earn each interviewee's confidence, trust and respect. Simply throwing a series of generalised assertions or snippets of gossip at the potential client and demanding that they confirm or deny them is unlikely to win you many friends. Treat your interviewee as you would an existing client, and broach the issues which you know to be problematic with diplomacy.

Creating the right impression

Don't be too gentle in your approach; if all your questions are anodyne, the prospective client may think you are as well. You need to show that you can be tactful but that, when circumstances demand it, you can also tackle the difficult issues. Much will depend on the management style of the people you are dealing with. Some organisations like the slightly combative approach, and deliberately look for advisers who are capable of challenging their assertions. This is what one managing director said of a firm's performance during the site visits:

> They sent along some very bright people, and their team made a lot more waves than anyone else's. We wanted to be challenged, even to the extent of putting some of our managers' backs up.

No-one will appoint a gratuitously aggressive team, but clients do want people who can show that they are sure of their ground and know how to use their knowledge to the client's advantage. Be friendly and polite, but remember that site visits are not about demonstrating how pleasant you are:

> The firm we appointed was prepared to point out weaknesses and ask searching questions. All the others were more concerned about creating a favourable impression by 'being nice'.

CREATING COMPETITIVE ADVANTAGE

Whatever the potential client may think, site visits should always be more than straightforward fact-finding sessions. Of course you should clarify the brief, supplement your knowledge of what is required and ask about the wider context in which the requirement has arisen. But most of all you should seek to use site visits as opportunities for demonstrating that you will make a productive contribution if appointed.

That's easy to say. How do you actually make it happen?

Taking the initiative

One of the most effective ways for any potential business adviser to think about site visits is to regard them as mini-consultancy assignments. That is, if you are told about a particular issue or problem – there will always be one, because the tender would not be taking place otherwise – you should proffer an initial opinion or solution.

The word *initial* is important here. Some proposers will argue that the submission of good ideas before the process is over is asking for trouble: the prospective client may simply give your sensible suggestion to your competitors or, worse still, take your advice and the necessary action without your help. This can be a genuine problem in the public sector, where attempts to be helpful by extending the specification or suggesting a more effective approach may result in the organisation asking your competitors (or its in-house people) to quote on exactly what you have proposed. They are not necessarily doing this for sinister reasons; it is simply that public servants feel obliged to create a level playing field on which everyone quotes for precisely the same thing.

In these and every tender, however, there is always room for the initial recommendation and tentative solution. Let someone else quote on your idea if they want to: if it is your thinking, your solution and your approach, it is unlikely that another organisation will be able to produce the benefits in quite the same way. Moreover, we are not suggesting that you should – or can – propose a definitive answer to difficult questions on the spot. If you make an initial recommendation, it will by definition need to be further thought out and refined later on – that is, when you are in full possession of the facts after you've won the assignment.

More compelling still is that the expression of initial ideas immediately puts your competitors on the defensive. If the prospective client tells them what you suggested, they will be obliged to come up with a view without necessarily having considered the issue. The client may also silently ask himself why, if it was obvious to you, your competitors had not thought of it too. In short, you will have created a lead which everyone else will be obliged to follow.

For instance, the production director may tell you about the difficulties being experienced in housing large quantities of stock and spares. You could suggest that he looks into establishing a just-in-time method of manufacturing which would eliminate the need for building new warehouses. You might then follow this up with the finance director by pointing out the advantages of such an approach in terms of reduced stock provisions, improved cashflow and the capital gain which could be generated through the sale of surplus storage capacity.

There are an infinite number of possibilities. When the prospective client mentions an issue or a problem, have an initial discussion about his options. Allude to ways in which your other clients have tackled similar difficulties, and how you were able to help overcome them; talk about how you would help the company get to grips with the underlying flaws which have produced the problem in the first place. Do this and it will quickly become apparent that you know your field and can make the kind of contribution which is needed.

Using your findings

As with your desk research, make sure that you use the information you have gathered through the site visits. In a large tender, it is quite possible for proposers to spend hundreds of man-hours and thousands of pounds in airfares flying around the world, and then not to use what they have discovered. Others will make these strenuous efforts and fail to find out anything remotely useful – usually because they have interviewed the wrong people, asked irrelevant questions or have not actually listened to what they have been told.

It is not enough simply to turn up and think that your presence alone will tip the balance in your favour. Only by probing, listening and looking for opportunities to demonstrate that you can make a fresh contribution can you create a competitive advantage.

KEY POINTS

- Make certain that you arrange site visits if the potential client is expecting them; failure to do so will put you at a fundamental disadvantage.

- If you believe the schedule of visits proposed by the target is unrealistic or unnecessary, tactfully say so and explain why – this may be a deliberate test of your willingness to challenge.

- Where you have not been invited to organise visits, discuss the brief with your contact over the 'phone and try to convince him to change his mind.

- Exercise caution in the number of interviews you ask for; too many site visits will irritate the decision-makers and be perceived as bad management.

- Be selective when deciding whom to interview; make sure that the people you visit can provide you with a genuine insight into their organisation's expectations, objectives and ambitions.

- Clarify the brief and use each interview to establish what the decision-makers need on a point-by-point basis; indicate any omissions or suggest constructive ways in which individual issues might be tackled differently.

- Send an agenda in advance of major or complex visits, but never submit a list of standard issues or questions; hold interviews at the potential client's premises, and try to avoid social settings.

- In no site visit should the numbers of your team exceed those of the potential client, while everyone who attends should have a clear reason for being there and an opportunity to contribute.

- Don't be too rigid about the structure of your discussions, but make sure that your questioning is polite, tactful on sensitive issues and at all times relevant to the tender.

- Where possible, provide your interviewees with initial opinions and recommendations; this will demonstrate that you can make a contribution to the potential client's business.

- Use site visits to discuss the target's needs and circumstances rather than your own credentials or attributes, and make sure that the key issues and other findings are fully addressed in your proposal.

7

FINALISING THE STRATEGY

MAKING DECISIONS

With the research and site visits over, you will at last be in a position to begin formulating your key proposal propositions. They may not simply fall into place; further work will be required to test hypotheses and define the factors which will create differentiation for your firm.

Then you will have to settle on a price. Can you convince the potential client that the fee proposal represents value for money; will it be perceived as credible; and how far should you be prepared to negotiate?

TESTING HYPOTHESES

The critical success factors matrix drawn up after your initial brainstorming session should by now have evolved into a series of hypotheses. These should begin to provide a clear indication of where you stand in the eyes of the prospective client and in relation to your competitors.

If, for instance, the matrix shows that your firm is comparatively weak in terms of its ability to meet the international requirements of the assignment, you will know that special effort will be needed to reassure the decision-makers that you have found an effective means of tackling the issue. Where the matrix suggests that your understanding of the organisation is stronger than that of the other firms, you will know that you need to emphasise this in the document or presentation.

Your assessment of strengths and weaknesses – and the ideas which have evolved from it – is bound to be speculative; you may not know whether the hypotheses are right until the end of the process. But you can at least test whether they make sense.

Brainstorming

Hold an open session in which everyone's ideas are fully discussed. No matter how unorthodox the suggestions at this stage, make sure that each team member is given the opportunity to contribute.

When you have compiled a list of the best ideas, review each one and decide whether they need to be developed further. For example, you may require further evidence to support an assertion or illustrate your approach.

Feedback from colleagues

Now ask for the views of your colleagues who have not been involved in the proposal (some large organisations regularly required to tender for work will have formal panels of 'wise men' for precisely this purpose). What do they make of the line you are proposing to take?

Many proposers will not involve their colleagues until they are ready to run through the presentation. This is too late: you will probably have submitted your document by this stage and you cannot start overturning everything you have done up until this point. The logistics of the process militate against it (is there, for instance, time to change all the slides?), and it is likely to damage the team's confidence.

Summarise the team's ideas on a sheet of paper and circulate it among those of your colleagues who have some knowledge of the potential client or its industry. Do they think you have successfully addressed the key issues? Which areas have you missed out? Do your propositions correspond to what the organisation is likely to be looking for in the current climate?

Encourage them to be honest and to suggest alternatives where appropriate. Give them a copy of the invitation to tender, too, and ask them whether they feel your response adequately addresses the brief. Since they have not been involved in the process up until now, their objectivity is likely to be valuable.

Feedback from contacts

Don't forget the people you saw during the research phase. If, for example, you spoke to ex-employees of the organisation, outline your thinking for the proposal and get them to give you their views. Do they think your ideas are likely to be well received? Are they perhaps too controversial – or too bland?

You might also consider going back to some of the analysts or other market commentators you interviewed. In the light of market conditions, how do they think your approach would help the organisation to address or capitalise on an important development in its sector? Do your ideas get to the heart of the problem, or might they be perceived as superficial?

Be careful about how much you reveal about your approach; after all, you don't know who else they might be talking to. Nevertheless, their views can be very helpful in deciding whether you are on the right track.

Feedback from the potential client

Prospective clients will often be willing to discuss your approach informally before you submit the document. They might do this just to be helpful or, for example, because one of the decision-makers has close personal links with your firm – perhaps it was this individual who was originally responsible for placing you on the tender list. (In such cases, you will nearly always find that his or her colleagues have equally close links with your competitors.)

Of course, you might discover that this form of cooperation is only being extended to a competitor. This is unlikely to be critical; it may be that their ally within the organisation will exercise little influence over the final decision or cannot reliably tell them whether their proposal hits the mark more accurately than any other.

It may be that you can ask someone in the organisation to review an early draft of the document. Perhaps you have established a good rapport with one of the decision-makers during the site visits, and are confident that he or she will not regard the request as inappropriate.

In tenders where you believe a direct invitation of this sort would be imprudent, you may be able to engineer a pretext on which to elicit a response. For example, you might suggest that your contact reviews a specific section, in order perhaps to clarify or debate a technical point. You should be able to use this as an opportunity to broaden the discussion.

Such stratagems, however, require careful judgement. Some decision-makers may regard any attempt to solicit unofficial cooperation as simply unethical.

FORMULATING KEY MESSAGES

When you have finished gathering intelligence, you need to formulate and finalise your key messages.

Get together again with the team and review your hypotheses in the light of any new information. Do your ideas still stand up? Are there any issues which have been omitted?

Go back to the brief and consider what this says about the decision-makers' priorities and expectations. Which are the issues they will regard as most important? From the evidence of the site visits and your subsequent discussions, what are the major preoccupations?

This is the stage where you also need to consider any hidden agendas. You may decide that you want to emphasise certain points because your research leads you to believe they address the areas which really concern the organisation, even if for some reason these concerns have not been made explicit.

Consider too the issues which your competitors are likely to focus on. Decide how you will defend any perceived weaknesses and how you might neutralise their strengths.

DIFFERENTIATORS

When you have devised the key messages, you need to ensure they will create genuine differentiation for your firm.

Many proposers still make the mistake of thinking that effective differentiation can be achieved by advertising the firm's intrinsic attributes: the number of offices, for example, or the number of staff; the range of expertise and clients, and track record on comparable assignments. But as we explained in Chapter 4, while these characteristics may help to persuade the decision-makers that you are *qualified* to do the job, this alone won't convince them that they want to work with you.

Consider what the buyers of professional services say. Here is one senior executive's view:

> The firm which won the tender focused on our real needs and put forward an approach which was specific to our business. The losing firm relied instead on the size of their organisation and the depth of their resources – that is, that they were simply bigger than any of their competitors and, therefore, the best firm for the job. This didn't tell us anything about how they would meet our requirements or give the value we were looking for.

So does the secret of differentiation lie in ensuring that you have a unique approach to the assignment? Not entirely. Here is another buyer's view:

> Methodologies were not a differentiating factor between firms, and I wouldn't be able to tell the difference between a good and a bad methodology anyway. The successful tenderer got the contract because they were able to articulate the benefits of their particular

approach. The methodology itself wasn't the point; what mattered was how it was going to help our organisation achieve its objectives.

This is not to say that methodology doesn't matter. In every proposal, you need to be clear about how you intend to tackle the job. But only rarely will the process itself be a key factor; however technical or complex the requirement, you must spell out what your approach will deliver.

What makes you different?

It is not uncommon to find the last page of many invitations to tender asking you to define what makes you different from your competitors. Don't take the question too literally; any sentence which begins, 'We are different because . . .' is likely to be followed by a rather embarrassing series of grandiloquent claims. In any case, being different for its own sake isn't enough.

Reinterpret the question to address the issue that lies behind it. What potential clients really want to know is how your appointment is going to make a difference to *their* organisation – in effect, how they will benefit from your involvement. If you answer that question instead, you will be able to highlight the advantages which your ideas and approach will bring.

You can also talk about credentials in terms of benefits. Your firm may be the world's largest provider of whatever the organisation needs but, as we know, this in itself is unlikely to be enough to secure your appointment. Think about how this unrivalled resource and experience is relevant, and tailor your claims accordingly. For instance:

The services of a global firm which will give you:

- access to the advice of locally-based technical specialists in every territory of the world in which you operate;
- the ability to draw on industry expertise relevant to your operating subsidiaries in each country.

This is not, however, the whole story; the following section explains how, having begun to express credentials in this way, you need to adapt them further in order to demonstrate how your resources will create advantage for the potential client. But practise the technique of turning credentials into benefits; the discipline is a good one because it will help you to think about your own firm in a new way.

Developing differentiating factors

Fig. 7.1 gives an example of a matrix which can be helpful in defining key points of differentiation. In this case, the matrix could have been prepared by a major law firm in response to a tender from a public company.

The left-hand column sets out a number of issues identified from the invitation to tender, desk research and site visits. Some constitute the basic requirements which initially led the organisation to ask for a proposal; others represent the law firm's own interpretation of what the prospective client needs. The second column sets out how the firm's services and resources will be deployed to address each need and issue, while the third summarises how each feature of the service will deliver a benefit for the organisation.

This matrix is a tool to help the proposal team define selling messages, each of which will need to be fully developed in the document or presentation. It will be invaluable for several reasons.

It should capture the essence of your proposal. If having completed the first column you can't finish the others, you will know that something is amiss. It will not do your firm any good if your document identifies a long series of needs which you cannot meet, or for which you cannot define a genuine benefit. The third column of the matrix is especially helpful in this respect, because it should tell you whether the distinguishing features are likely to create real advantages, or will merely be perceived as gimmicks.

Try to take a dispassionate view of the matrix, and ask yourself whether the key elements strike you as credible. If they don't, the potential client will probably be sceptical too.

Then consider whether the target is likely to see a similar set of

Issue	Feature of our service	Benefit to client
Client alienated by existing advisers' fee rates and uncertainty over costs	Monthly statements tracking time spent against forecast Different fee bands used to reflect complexity of the work	Better able to control and monitor costs More cost-effective use of law firm
Need for fast response and access to legal expertise at all times	Back-up for each partner/fee earner	Deadlines always met
Need for guidance on how other companies deal with regulatory issues within the industry (eg environmental)	Partner/fee earners with industry experience	Pro-active advice on best practice within the industry
Need to reduce litigation costs	Commercial approach to litigation (eg illustrated through case studies)	Commercial objectives achieved
In-house lawyers have to deal with fluctuating workload on routine matters	Offer to provide lower-level support to in-house team	Costs reduced by keeping staffing levels in-house to a minimum

Figure 7.1   Issues, features and benefits

messages from your competitors. Do the second and third columns suggest that you have applied some hard thinking to how you are going to meet the potential client's needs, or do they come across as prosaic and predictable? Are the key messages, service features and benefits something that only your firm could deliver, or do they convey an approach which might be adopted by any of the other contenders?

Remember: the way you approach an assignment takes second place to what it delivers for the client. Many organisations cannot tell the difference between one methodology and another – and, just as often, aren't remotely interested. Only by emphasising the benefits of their approach can proposers succeed in creating a winning advantage.

VALUE FOR MONEY

The most concrete differentiating factor of any proposal is the price of the services on offer. In the economic conditions of the last few years, pricing may have assumed a more and more dominant role in tender decisions as suppliers have been increasingly willing to discount their rates.

Pressure on price is no surprise; the recession has created a buyers' market in most sectors of the economy. The difficulty is that for many businesses, being compelled to compete *solely* on price could spell commercial death in the long run. It is essential for most firms which make their living from selling technical or professional expertise to be able to convince buyers that a quality differential is worth paying for. When expertise is reduced to the status of mere commodity, it is not only margins that crumble; these are people businesses where staff morale and the ability to attract high-calibre recruits is imperative for survival.

It is important, however, to keep pricing in perspective. Buyers will not consider the fee in a complete vacuum because they know – however subconsciously – that it is seldom in their best interests to do so. Assessments of cost will usually be based on a variety of factors, which together help to shape the concept of value for money.

So how do potential clients decide what constitutes value for money? Below are some of the factors they will tend to take into account.

Team structure

The balance between senior and more junior resources can be of the greatest importance.

Where an assignment requires different levels of skills and experience, the organisation is unlikely to be prepared to pay high rates across the board. This may seem self-evident, but it is surprising how many firms fail to offer differential billing rates which reflect the types of work for which they are proposing. In an increasingly competitive marketplace, clients want to see a distinction made between high- and low-value work:

> We're no longer willing to pay for expensive lower-level resource for work which, although it has a part to play, we do not value highly. We want to see our advisers' fees reflecting the nature of the task they're being asked to perform.

By the same token, buyers will be sceptical about composite hourly charges for your team (i.e. a single rate for every individual involved, irrespective of their experience). It raises too many unanswered questions about the cost-effectiveness with which the work will be handled:

> A composite rate may appear to be good value when judged in terms of a senior professional's normal charge-out rate. But you often find that, because the level of senior involvement will in practice be comparatively limited, you're paying far too high a rate for junior resources. In my view, anyone who accepts such an arrangement is asking to get a bad deal. They're also taking a risk that important work will be performed by inexperienced people so that the recovery rate is protected.

The basic rule is straightforward. When proposing a fee, make sure that the resources you intend to deploy reflect the complexity and importance of the work involved. You will run into trouble if they don't:

> I don't mind paying top rates for advice which is central to the business's future, but I won't pay £150 an hour for a trainee to fill out tax returns.

Management skills

How you intend to manage the team can also affect the potential client's perceptions of value for money. Where you are billing purely on time, he or she needs to be convinced that effort will not be wasted on activities which do not contribute to meeting the objectives of the assignment.

In many proposal situations, a firm will be asked to estimate the first year's charges. Some respond to this request by providing an aggregate fee figure for the year and a summary of hourly charge-out rates for each grade of individual involved. Critically, however, they fail to provide a breakdown of the total hours key individuals will commit to the project. As a result, the organisation has no way of knowing whether the total fee is set at the right level – because there is no information on who will be doing what and for how long over the 12-month period.

Accountability for fees is all-important: not just in proposing an initial figure, but also in demonstrating your ability to manage the fee relationship over a period of time. You may convince the decision-makers that your estimate is appropriate in the current circumstances; but how can they be sure that your charges will continue to represent value for money into the future?

Make clear that you intend to set in place a range of procedures which will enable the potential client to monitor and assess fee levels regularly. These might include the offer to provide monthly statements of work in progress and hours committed to date on a project-by-project basis. You could also include a sample invoice in an appendix to the proposal document, showing how you set out the charges for work performed and the seniority (and cost) of the individuals involved in a typical fee note.

The psychology of negotiating and managing the fee relationship is a discipline in its own right. Service providers often pay little attention to their invoicing, lumping together all kinds of high and low value advice in a single fee note entitled, for instance, 'routine tax compliance'. This does not help the client assess whether the concomitant charges represent value for money, and worse still may undermine the goodwill you have built up from doing a good job. If you say the advice was 'routine', don't be surprised if you are taken at your word. It may be that your advice has actually saved the client a large tax bill but, if that cannot be deciphered from the invoice or a covering letter, you will have squandered your advantage.

Don't wait until you have won the work to show that you will manage the fee relationship effectively. Make clear from the outset that you understand costs need to be controlled, and that you are fully prepared to be held accountable for fees.

In an international assignment, perhaps involving several teams and offices, the prospective client has to be convinced that the subsidiaries will be as accountable as you are. According to one American-based executive:

> We were by no means sure that the US arm of the firm would be able to exert sufficient pressure on its operations in other countries to keep fees down. In essence, we didn't believe that the US partners would be able to crack the whip firmly enough with their counterparts overseas.

Again, you need to discuss the measures you will put in place to ensure that, wherever your service is required, costs will be managed effectively.

Resources

There is no reason on earth why any potential client should help meet the cost of your overhead unless he is going to benefit from it. You may have offices and experts in every major country of the world, but these will be irrelevant if you are being asked to propose for the conveyance of a factory which is next door to the prospective client's existing premises. If anything, size and depth of resources will lead clients to expect economies of scale – not a loading of the fee to pay for their upkeep.

The cost of change

The change from one set of advisers to another usually involves disruption and, therefore, additional cost. Most organisations will be aware of this and, in many cases, will be able to quantify that cost in terms of the man-hours required internally to get the new advisers up to speed – especially if they have experienced a change of advisers before.

Given that the cost of change can be significant, the organisation needs to be reassured that it will still derive a net benefit from switching to your firm and that, irrespective of your overall contribution, the financial implications are acceptable.

The financial penalty involved can be eased to some extent if you offer to absorb the time costs of establishing the relationship or, perhaps, discount the fee in the first year by way of compensation. Whatever level you have pitched the fee, the decision-makers will have to be convinced that the opportunity and direct costs associated with bringing in new advisers is worth paying. Quite often, the prospective client will decide that it isn't:

> We didn't consider that the cost of change would be sufficiently offset by the saving in fee we would have gained even by appointing the lowest-bidding firm.

This reluctance to pay for change will, of course, be helpful to any incumbent firm. But no incumbent should rely on the fact that change is expensive; it is only one of several factors involved and, if your firm is perceived as the problem, the cost-benefit equation will almost certainly work against you.

Prospective clients will have different ideas about what represents value for money. In the public sector, for instance, the best value for money tends to be defined as the lowest possible price for a given set of requirements. In this and every other market, however, buyers need to know that your fee reflects only what you are being asked to do, that the fee relationship will be effectively controlled, and that the people and resources you assign to the job are appropriate to the task in hand. Get this formula right and you will find it considerably easier to convince a target that your service will be cost-effective:

> Our approach is to see whether we are being offered the right time commitment, quality and mix of people. If these are fine, the fee will become very much a secondary consideration.

PROPOSING A FEE

Deciding on the fee is never straightforward, but take heart from the fact that your competitors find it equally problematic. Moreover, it's too easy to convince yourself as the proposal develops that, in the end, it will all come down to price. Try to resist this inclination – you might be pleasantly surprised.

In a tight market, organisations know that the process of issuing an invitation to tender is by its nature likely to encourage competitive pricing among those asked to respond. At the same time, experience suggests that it is rare for a bid to be accepted if the prospective client is being offered a rock-bottom or loss-leading price. Most prospective clients will be highly suspicious of a 'lowball'. A senior executive explains why:

> When one of the firms came in with a lowballed fee some 50 per cent below all the others, I and my directors saw it as a cynical attempt to get the job. It also raised serious doubts about the level of service and commitment to the work over the longer term; they couldn't possibly have done all the things we wanted at those prices, and I suspect we would either have been made to pay more later on or suffered poor service if they'd been appointed. Frankly, their fee proposal insulted our intelligence.

Lowballing for its own sake can be particularly damaging where a firm is proposing for reappointment:

> The incumbent firm's fee was way below everyone else's, which immediately set off a series of very loud alarm bells. We thought they would cut corners and do a lot less in future years than they had in the past. Or it meant they intended to cut down on the senior time and give the

work to inexperienced people. And if they could afford to drop their charges like this, it suggested we'd been exploited over a long time. Basically, we just saw their proposed fee as a desperate, last-ditch attempt to save the work.

Quite often, an organisation will use the fee issue as a pretext for securing a new or improved approach from its existing advisers. So the incumbent firm will propose a lower fee level without making any other changes and find, much to its chagrin, that it still loses the work. Other clients, of course, will do it the other way around; they will complain about the approach, when what they really want is a lower fee for exactly the same work.

It is understandable that proposers become cynical about prospective clients' motives for putting work out to tender. It is not unknown for some organisations simply to lie about the relative importance of the fee. They might claim that the price of the service is secondary to the benefits which it delivers but, in the end, will opt for the cheapest bid.

Fortunately, such cases are rare. More often, the process can be made to work to a proposer's advantage. If your firm can put forward a compelling proposition, the target may well be convinced that a higher price is worth paying:

> The Board initiated the tender because they thought it would enable us to get a cheaper service. Such was the quality of the winning firm's proposal, however, that price didn't figure at all in the final decision.

Deciding on a figure

The site visits and other research should have given you a reasonable idea of the fee level which is likely to be acceptable to the target. The issue should be discussed with your team and, where appropriate, with other colleagues.

Leaving aside lowballing, which is designed to win the work at any price, you may decide to propose a low fee as an investment. There could be several reasons for this: you may want the work because it is strategically important for your firm (perhaps it will get you into a new market sector, or you want to protect market share); you need the client, rather than the work (because the organisation is a prestigious one); or you just need the work (because your team has spare capacity). They are all legitimate commercial reasons for proposing a low fee, but remember the price still has to be credible.

Alternatively, you may know that the assignment will lead to other and more lucrative work. You can't say that to the potential client, of course; most buyers will feel uneasy about a service provider which is losing money on their business and, in all cases, would react badly to the suspicion of an implicit quid pro quo which morally obliged them to award other contracts in order to make up the difference. Do it as a loss-leader if you want to, but make sure that you have an explanation prepared for the reduced fee.

Occasionally, you may even decide that you have no choice but to submit a much higher fee than the potential client is expecting. That could be because the organisation is itself being unrealistic about what can be achieved for a particular price. In these circumstances, propose your fee, but don't wait to be asked to explain it. Make it clear from the outset why you believe the organisation's objectives cannot be met for a lower price and how the figure, though higher than expected, still represents value for money.

Is your fee credible?

Large or small, credibility is key to every fee proposal. We have already mentioned some of the reasons why a target may be sceptical: poor team management skills, an inability to control overseas operations and so on. What counts in the last analysis is the provision of a sound and logical foundation for your charging structure.

This means, for instance, that a low fee proposal can succeed if it is clear that you will be able to do the work for that price. This is how one client reacted to a very low tender figure:

The winning firm's fee was considerably lower than those of their competitors. We gave them the job because we were convinced from their more efficient approach that they would be able to do the work in considerably less time than anyone else.

At all costs, you must avoid unexplained, last-minute reductions. They are seldom well received:

> We were at the last stage, and one of the three firms suddenly cut their fee by 45 per cent because they realised they were way out of line with the others. It completely blew their credibility and was regarded by my colleagues as a total fiasco. It wasn't very bright of them: that we'd invited them through to the last round should have made them realise that we were actually quite interested in finding out why they'd priced the job as they did. If the fee had been our only criterion, they'd have been dropped from the tender as soon as they submitted their proposal.

In another case:

> One of the firms offered a second and much lower fee. The hours they were proposing to spend on the job, though, remained exactly the same. This clearly implied that they were willing to lose money on the assignment, and we all felt they should have spoken to us honestly about that first. We'd have been more than happy to have discussed their reasons without thinking any the less of them. As it was, the *fait accompli* raised doubts about their credibility.

The best policy is not to make savage cuts in your fee proposal at all. If you have presented a strong case for your charges, you should be equipped to defend them under any amount of fire. Last-minute reductions always look bad, and it's difficult to find a credible reason to justify them without appearing to the decision-makers to have made a critical mistake somewhere along the line. Arguments such as 'we overestimated the number of hours required' or 'we've looked again at the work and decided that more of it can be done at junior level' always come across as lame and self-conscious.

Leaving room for negotiation

Some buyers relish the idea of extended fee negotiations; some are horrified by the idea of a 'Dutch auction'; and some are prepared to accept the first figure offered provided it is backed by sound logic.

The culture of the organisation will tell you a great deal about their likely reaction to your fee proposal. There are no hard and fast rules, but if, for instance, you are tendering to a highly entrepreneurial, owner-managed business, it would probably be unrealistic to expect the key decision-maker not to want to negotiate a reduction.

In some cases – as long as it doesn't knock you out of the running to begin with – you may try to anticipate this by initially proposing a fee which is higher than necessary. In others, where you wish to protect the original figure as long as you can, you may decide to absorb an element of your costs in areas such as travel or recharges.

Of course, you will be more inclined to cut the fee if you know it is likely to mean the difference between winning or losing. In these circumstances, you can signal your flexibility by saying that you are happy to explore with the target 'any areas where a reduction in cost can be achieved'. This is straightforward code for 'we're willing to reduce the price as long as you're willing to provide us with a genuine reason why we should do it'.

There is a school of thought which suggests that in these circumstances you can try: 'We would be loath to lose this assignment on the basis of fee alone'. In our view, this carries too great a risk of being misinterpreted as an open invitation for the target to knock your fee down irrespective of how competitive it is. Other prospective clients might simply regard it as crass, or defensive, or both.

In practice, there is seldom a need to resort to such methods. You can, for instance, hold out the carrot of fee reductions for retained work in future years on the basis that, with the learning curve complete, you will be much more efficient in your role. You might, in addition, offer to absorb any future inflationary increases in your charge-out rates over an agreed period, or propose to tackle aspects of the assignment on a success or contingency fee basis (but only where you're sure of achieving satisfactory results).

You can also offer incentives. These could include, for instance, a 'subsidised' or even free additional service, or a series of in-house seminars on key issues for the potential client's staff.

Remember that successful pricing and differentiation is all about having the courage of your convictions. If you think your proposal is based on accurate research, sound business assumptions, quality ideas and logical pricing, don't allow yourself to be talked too easily out of your approach – or your fee.

KEY POINTS

- Hold a team session to agree the key elements of your proposal, but make sure each one is supported by genuine evidence and meets a specific need.

- Discuss your ideas with colleagues and contacts and, before and after the drafting stage, also take every opportunity to gain feedback from the potential client.

- Prioritise your key points and messages to reflect the relative importance of the target's known and perceived requirements.

- Don't rely on methodologies or corporate credentials to create effective differentiation; focus instead on the benefits of your approach.

- Don't be too literal in answering the question 'What makes you different?'; reinterpret any such request as an opportunity to discuss the advantages your appointment will create.

- Using a matrix, relate the features of your service to the target's needs and define the benefits you will bring in each case.

- Make sure the differentiating factors look credible, and cannot be viewed as gimmicks.

- Perceptions of value for money are based on more than the price; they are likely to be influenced by the quality of the team, their management skills and the cost of changing suppliers.

- A dramatic lowball seldom pays off; the fee proposal must be credible.

- Always set out a logical and comprehensive basis for your charging structure; do not give prospective clients an opportunity to perform the wrong calculations.

- Never resort to last-minute, unexplained fee reductions; provide a reason for any discounts and find a way to accommodate the target's budgetary concerns through other means.

- Be prepared and leave room for negotiations, but stand by the quality and pricing fundamentals of your proposal.

8

THE PROPOSAL DOCUMENT

OBJECTIVES OF THE DOCUMENT

Nearly every proposal requires some form of document. Yet attitudes to this aspect of the process reveal a curious anomaly. Experienced proposers are often sceptical about the importance of the written part of the proposal. Some maintain that it is rarely decisive in determining the outcome of a tender; or that it is capable of losing a tender, but never of winning one. Others insist that proposal documents are seldom actually read at all, or at least not by the key decision makers.

Contrast these views with what actually happens in practice. The drafting and production of the document will absorb more of the proposal team's time and energy than any other part of the process, often at the expense of equally – or more – critical activities. Indeed, you often find that the term 'proposal' is used to describe only the written report – as if there were nothing more to the entire event than merely sending off a sheaf of pages.

As we have tried to demonstrate throughout this book, *every* stage of a proposal is important – from how you respond to the invitation through to the research and conduct of initial meetings and beyond. None should be neglected. But – and here is the anomaly – if proposal teams have little faith in the power of the document to influence the result, why do they spend inordinate amounts of time on it?

Proposals tend to be reactive by nature – they usually start with somebody asking you to respond. Therefore it is easy to slip into a reactive frame of mind in conducting the exercise. Naturally, it is tempting to concentrate on the part of the process which requires you to deliver a tangible product rather than the numerous imponderables which form part of any proposal (how do we get closer to the prospective client; who else should we be talking to; do we need to reinterpret the brief in the light of what has been said at the meetings?).

The temptation should be firmly resisted. Allowing yourself to be subsumed by the mechanics of producing the document, instead of keeping a critical eye on the key factors which will decide the outcome, is a common but often fatal error. If, for example, you think you don't have enough time to conduct all the meetings you would like because of the pressures of getting the document out, you can be sure that the management of the exercise has gone awry.

Having put the document into perspective, it is still important to understand what role it fulfils and how it can advance your cause. It is true that in most instances, the written part of the proposal is unlikely to be decisive on its own. In order to put their trust in you – which is what selecting advisers amounts to – decision makers want to ask questions and probe potential weaknesses. The document, as a form of one-way communication, gives them no opportunity to do that. So, a lacklustre or unconvincing performance at the presentation will easily vitiate a good piece of written work. But the reverse also applies. Although there are exceptions, a bravura presentation is unlikely to redeem your chances of success if the team's credibility has already been damaged by a poorly conceived or badly written document.

It therefore must be right to treat every aspect of your communications with the prospective client – from the site visits and informal conversations through to the document and presentation – as equal parts of an integrated campaign, rather than as discrete idioms competing for priority, to be promoted or relegated at will.

Why do nearly all tenders require the submission of a document? It depends on the circumstances and on the organisation. The most common reasons are listed below:

To examine the credentials of the competing firms

Documentary evidence is usually required to make detailed comparisons between the competing firms' experience, resources and infrastructure. The presentation is unlikely to allow time for a disquisition on these subjects from the proposers (quite apart from the fact that the selection panel would be disinclined to listen to it). The document stage can also be used to filter out less suitable contenders, in order to arrive at a manageable number who will subsequently be invited to put their case in person.

To learn about the backgrounds and biographical details of the team members

This is likely to count for more with the decision-makers than general credentials about the firm, but again it is usually inappropriate to devote precious presentation time to the exposition of career histories. The document provides a con-venient outlet for this kind of information.

To make a comparison of proposed fees and costs

Firms are usually required to include information relating to their proposed fees in the document. Inclusion of financial details will allow time for the prospective client to digest the material and possibly to prepare questions for the presentation.

To gain an insight into how the team will perform on the assignment

Assuming that each team's experience, expertise and ability to do the job appear to be roughly equal, it is this aspect which the potential client will regard as the most important – and find the most revealing. How well have they understood our business and our objectives? How do they propose to manage the assignment –

do their suggestions fit well with our culture or structure? Will it provide us with the level and quality of support we need? Have they tailored their approach to our specific needs? What are likely to be the benefits of hiring them? No proposal document can fail, consciously or inadvertently, to provide at least partial answers to these questions. And the quality of the answers will have a crucial bearing on the outcome.

It is not only the substance of the document, however, which will give the recipient an insight into how effectively the assignment will be handled. He or she may be able to infer a great deal from its structure, style and even appearance.

For example, going to the trouble of producing a glossy, expensive-looking volume could be favourably received by some organisations, which may interpret the effort and expense as a sign of commitment and enthusiasm to do the job. But the same style of presentation may cause apprehension – or even irritation – if the organisation is one which prides itself on keeping costs to an absolute minimum. The recipients will be asking themselves: will this firm have a cavalier approach to charging fees and incurring costs on my organisation's behalf? Have they failed to understand the culture of the organisation to which they are proposing? Such concerns are unlikely to be critical in their own right, but could well fatally reinforce unfavourable impressions which have already been created.

Similarly, a lengthy document which explores every aspect of the assignment is more likely to appeal to an organisation whose decision-makers are 'academicians' with an eye for detail than a company run by, say, a seat-of-the-pants entrepreneur who only wants to know the broad sweep of your proposals. The sensitivity with which you handle these issues during the proposal is bound to be regarded as an indication of how the relationship is likely to develop if you are awarded the work.

The importance of good style should never be underestimated. Of course, the prospective client is not likely to be formally assess-ing the quality of English in your document; you won't find any reference to this requirement in the brief and it won't be one of the official selection criteria. Nor is it probable that inelegant prose or bad syntax will offend the decision makers' aesthetic sensibilities: you are not tendering for the job of Poet Laureate. But a carelessly written document will suggest to the reader that you may be careless in other respects – such as in carrying out the assignment.

The real danger in bad prose, however, lies in its subliminal effects on the reader. Decision makers are under as much time pressure as proposers: and the task of having to read maybe four or five proposals is just as onerous as having to write *one*. Readers may not be consciously aware of the fact they are suffering from exposure to bad prose, but they will certainly be feeling the symptoms. Poor concentration, re-reading sentences frequently, a sense of having to guess at the meaning, the rapid onset of fatigue and finding excuses to do something else are certain to be among them.

In essence, bad style is about lack of clarity. The link between content and style is an intimate one, and clouded prose will always suggest muddled thinking. The quality of English in your document will not fail to leave an impression on the readers; it will influence their perception of you and your fitness to do the job.

So much for the function of the document from the client's perspective. But the process of preparing it should also play an important part in crystallising the thinking of the proposal team and ensuring that your firm advances its case most effectively. Even if you are certain about how the assignment should be tackled, who should be on the team and why your firm should succeed in the tender, the process of writing and reviewing the written word tends to bring these issues into sharper focus – and often brings previously submerged problems to the surface. It is always easy to talk, but committing thoughts to paper will often force you to re-examine your ideas and claims. This does not mean, however, that you should start writing the document at the earliest opportunity – quite the contrary, as we argue below. It does mean that anyone who is involved in drafting the document must be prepared to redraft and refine the text repeatedly as the messages are honed and sharpened.

DRAFTING AND PRODUCTION

The principles which underpin good management of the proposal process as a whole – developing a critical path, defining roles for team members, appointing a dedicated proposal manager and so on – apply with the greatest force to the preparation of the document. And it is in connection with the document that your management skills, not to say patience, are often tested most severely.

At the beginning of the proposal, you will of course find out the date by which the document will need to be submitted. Working backwards from that date, you need to establish a series of subsidiary deadlines corresponding to key production and drafting phases. On the production side, the exigencies of the timetable will be greater if the document is to be externally typeset and printed. With recent advances in desk-top publishing technology this requirement is becoming increasingly irrelevant for most proposers, but even so extra time must be allowed for the processing of graphics and, of course, photographs. If you intend to use printed covers, it also makes sense to set their production in train as early as you can so that there will be enough time to consider alternative lay-outs and designs.

Decide who in your firm needs to see the document, and at which stages of its development. Even in a small proposal, you should ensure that a quality control function is built into the process. During the preparatory stages, colleagues should be invited to review the content and express a view on the fundamentals, such as the intended approach to the assignment and the fee. And before sending it off, make sure that you get a fresh pair of eyes to proof-read it; somebody else (preferably not a team member) should be assigned the task of ensuring that factual narrative is correct and consistent. All these tasks have to be incorporated into the timetable. If you are able to appoint a proposal manager to handle the logistics of document preparation, so much the better; but in any event, the key point is that a critical path for the document should be in place long before the writing starts.

Dealing with the logistics is usually child's play compared with the much more problematic task of managing the drafting process. Here there are two golden rules, both of which are obvious enough yet nearly always ignored: do not convert your thoughts into prose until you have a clear idea of what your thoughts are; and appoint only one person to coordinate the drafting.

Proposers are often tempted to begin drafting as early as possible. Some may believe that it shows they are thinking ahead; others perhaps just want to avoid the usual trap of leaving everything to the last moment. Far from being a sign of efficiency, however, premature attempts at drafting usually turn out to be an extravagant waste of time – at a stage when you can least afford it.

In the previous section, we said that committing your ideas to paper will force you to re-examine them, and therefore continual revision of the text is inevitable. But the purpose of the revising process is to help fine-tune the messages and improve the quality of the prose, not to rehearse the debate about how the document should be tackled and which ideas and approaches it should contain – that can be done much more effectively in front of a flipchart, using the techniques we outlined in the last chapter.

If you were building a house, you would presumably decide on the floor plan before you turned your attention to the lighting and decoration. The same applies when the edifice you are constructing is a proposal document. So begin with the floor plan, or synopsis. Consider the broad areas that need to be covered and roughly in which order. Share it with your colleagues. It is only after team members as a group have discussed the synopsis and agreed the approach on which it is based that you should think about drafting. When it comes to getting their contribution to specific sections, they will then understand the context in which they are being asked to supply material and how it is intended to fit with the rest of the text.

This brings us on to the second golden rule: many people may need to contribute to the document, but only one should be editor. Often it is best if the editor is given responsibility for drafting the entire document, having discussed the various sections individually with the relevant team members. Where this is not practical, the editor should persuade the other participants to concentrate on setting out the key points rather than attempting to draft finished prose. This is because it is much easier to convert basic notes or bullet points into a coherent passage than it is to rewrite dense text.

The drafting process must be tightly coordinated and controlled, with each writer 'reporting' to the editor rather than shuffling papers between themselves. Above all, do not let team members work on the draft in isolation from the editor. The result will not only be a mishmash of writing styles; the content itself will suffer. Invariably, you will find yourself with a draft which is in turn contradictory and repetitive; it will take longer to sort out than if the editor had written the whole thing from scratch. (The editor need not be a member of the assignment team. The only requirements are that he or she should be an excellent writer; is able to grasp the messages which the team wants to convey; and is willing to challenge assumptions or claims which do not stand up to critical scrutiny.)

Bear in mind that it is usually the most important proposals where the quality of the document is most at risk. Large proposals generally mean large teams; they also tend to capture the attention of senior colleagues who are not even on the team. And the more people who are involved, the harder it is likely to be to control the drafting process. These are circumstances where an authoritarian streak in the proposal leader will do more good than harm.

THE PATHOLOGIES OF PROPOSAL WRITING

Having had the opportunity to review a wide variety of proposal documents produced by companies operating in a diverse range of business sectors, our conclusion is that proposal writing is a medium in which firms seldom do themselves justice. The reasons for this are far from obvious. Most firms take the opportunity to win work very seriously, and are unstinting in committing the time and energy required to set out a convincing case on paper. Yet the end product is often not remotely commensurate with the effort and expense devoted to the exercise.

A number of explanations could be advanced to account for this phenomenon. Failure to manage the drafting process effectively, in the manner described in the previous section, is certainly a major factor. There are others.

Many businesses which are now obliged to compete regularly for work through competitive tenders are still uncomfortable with the process, and this shows clearly enough in their proposal writing. People who are down to earth and unaffected in conversation can easily become the epitome of presumptuousness and pomposity when required to express themselves on paper. And those who would in any other circumstance be capable of giving a straight-forward view on a subject on which they are expert often seem to be paralysed into confining themselves to platitudes and truisms if a written exposition of their ideas is needed.

Perhaps it is our system of education, with its lamentable failure to encourage the development of effective writing skills, which should take a share of the blame; or for that matter individual companies, which do not put sufficient emphasis on this area in their training programmes.

Whatever the reasons, most proposal documents contain significant weaknesses in structure, content and style. To compile a definitive taxonomy of these weaknesses would certainly require a book in itself, but it is worth highlighting the errors which occur most frequently – and those which most tend to irritate, confuse or distract the reader.

Structure and content

Ultimately it is impossible to draw a rigid distinction between structure, content and style – what appears to be a stylistic weakness may have its roots in the substance of the message and vice versa. However, the following problems tend to be associated more closely with the subject matter than the way it is expressed.

Boilerplate – and the curse of plagiarism

For those unfamiliar with the term, 'boilerplate' refers to standard, pre-prepared text which can be slotted into proposal documents. Some firms encourage the use of boilerplate on the grounds that producing a document from scratch amounts to a tiresome reinvention of the wheel, and that considerable time can be saved if proposers have at their disposal a 'library' of suitable passages and sections which can be conveniently resurrected as the need arises. Some also see it as a quality control mechanism: the pre-prepared text will presumably have been carefully written and edited; its use should at least help to ensure that proposal documents produced by different writers achieve a common standard.

If you have been asked to produce a credentials document, intended to do no more than outline the track record of the firm and give biographical details of its members, boilerplate is adequate – although even here there is usually an opportunity to tailor the material to the reader. In most written proposals, however, you are expected to go much further: the prospective client will want to know how you will approach the assignment and why you are qualified to do the job. It is here that the boilerplate technique breaks down.

In an effective document, all the sections should be mutually reinforcing: the same messages will come through when you are describing how you will tackle the job, what your firm's experience is, who you have selected for the team, how you will report to the client – even in the case studies, if you're using some. In other words, virtually all the material will need to be tailored to the specific objectives, requirements and circumstances of the assignment. The boilerplate will therefore need radical amendment: very often it will be less time consuming and more effective to produce a fresh draft. In practice, therefore, boilerplate has limited application.

Having standard text available is, however, infinitely preferable to letting teams plunder the firm's previous proposals. Lengthy passages will be faithfully reproduced without any regard for the fact that the context is completely different. The perpetrators may even start to think that if they plagiarise from one of the firm's winning efforts, success will be theirs too.

Remember, prospective clients are looking for evidence from your document that you have understood their needs, and that you can work together. Your cause will therefore not be advanced by serving up old material prepared for someone else. And worse, what you've done will be instantly transparent to the reader.

Focusing on the firm, not the client

The prospective client may have spent considerable time briefing you about the nature of the assignment, his or her organisation's objectives and the problems and challenges which it faces. When your proposal document arrives, the recipient turns to page one and reads:

> ABC & Co is a well established medium-sized City firm serving a wide range of clients in a range of industries. We have 27 partners and nearly 200 staff. In addition to our City office, we are represented in each region of the UK.

What would be your reaction if *you* were the prospective client? And how would you feel if you had to read four or five proposals which all started in the same way?

It is remarkable how often, even after extensive site visits and research, the proposal document hardly touches on the organisation for which it was written. Even if it does contain material which directly addresses its needs, this is frequently buried at the bottom of page 16 and, assuming the reader gets that far, he or she will have lost interest anyway. The sense of introspection this conveys will not help to convince the reader that you are thinking about the organisation's problems and how to solve them.

Failure to focus on the client is one of the most fundamental weaknesses to be found in proposal documents, and is among the most common. From the reader's standpoint, it is also one of the most conspicuous.

Regurgitation

Some proposers make sure that there is plenty of material about the client in their document by reproducing lengthy passages from the brief or repeating large chunks of what was said at the interviews. In Chapter 5 we referred to the tendency to produce detailed profiles on the tendering organisation which do not relate to the assignment or how you propose to tackle it. This can be almost as irritating as not writing about the client at all:

> One firm went to town on our company, providing an analysis of our financial performance and commentary on our market position. The trouble was that they didn't tell us anything we didn't already know – in fact, most of what they told us *we had already told them.* We had the feeling that we were wasting time in reading the proposal.

Reiterating what you have been told about the organisation is only appropriate if you can add your own knowledge, expertise and perspective to the subject. The reader will have no difficulty distinguishing between material which is being regurgitated from existing sources and information to which you have added value.

Features, not benefits

In setting out how it is intended that the assignment will be tackled, proposal teams often describe the characteristics of their approach in great detail without explaining what the potential client will gain as a result. Not unnaturally, the reader will assume that the team is more interested in the technicalities of its own service than helping the tendering organisation to meet its objectives. Moreover, key messages and differentiators will be blunted, or lost altogether.

The failure to elucidate benefits shows that the team has been unable to distinguish between means and ends from the decision-makers' viewpoint. A common example of a feature which masquerades as a benefit is the team's experience of working with similar clients in previous assignments:

> All members of our team have worked with clients in the pharmaceuticals sector. We will therefore be able to bring extensive industry expertise and experience to bear if appointed by your company.

The proposal team may believe that the advantages of having relevant industry expertise are self-evident, and that it is a major selling point. The prospective client, however, will want to know precisely how this capability will assist in meeting the objectives of the assignment. For instance, it might relevant in:

- analysing technical problems and expediting solutions
- reducing the amount of time the organisation needs to spend with the appointed team explaining the issues and helping them to prepare for the assignment
- providing comparisons with other companies in the sector
- introducing the decision-makers to key figures in the industry, or in other segments of the industry.

Depending on the goals of the organisation and the purpose of the tender, all, some or none of these potential benefits could be of value; and in any case, more detail will be required (which technical problems can be solved by using industry expertise? How will providing comparisons with other companies in the sector be helpful?). Thus, being able to offer industry expertise is not of intrinsic value to the prospective client; it is a (perhaps essential) means of achieving something else.

Preparing an issues, features and benefits matrix is a useful discipline in clarifying the linkages between the characteristics of your approach and the needs of the prospective client.

Irrelevance

Nobody charged with writing or contributing to a proposal document needs to be told that the submission should not include material which is irrelevant to the recipients, yet in practice this is a weakness which is difficult to eradicate. Reliance on boilerplate, insufficient control over the drafting process and weak editing are the chief causes.

The most common manifestation of irrelevance in proposal documents is covering ground which is not in the brief. Some firms cannot resist the temptation to describe a range of services and skills unrelated to the assignment for which they've been asked to tender, just in case the organisation might need them. Unless a list of additional services has been requested, it is better to avoid this practice. Your opportunity to cross-sell other parts of the firm will come once the assignment has been won.

Be on your guard against irrelevance creeping into the less prominent parts of the document. For example, documents which admirably stick to the point in describing how the assignment will be conducted often fall down in the descriptions of team members' biographies. It is not reassuring for the prospective client to read that the lead partner 'specialises in multinational assignments for leading plcs' when he or she is the director of a small owner-managed business with no interests overseas.

Repetition

The need to avoid repetition is equally obvious. The solution again lies in ensuring that drafting is effectively coordinated and that the editor is in control. While it should be a straightforward matter to eliminate the most conspicuous instances of duplication, vigilance is needed to ensure that the same form of words are not repeated in different contexts.

Let us assume that one of the advantages which your firm offers is that you have offices at every location where the prospective client operates. You may find yourself pointing this out on virtually every page of the document: in the section covering your approach to the assignment ('one of the key aspects of our approach is that your operations will be served by locally based directors and staff'); in the section on the team; under fees ('our use of local offices will ensure a cost-effective service'); in the description of the firm's resources and infrastructure; and, of course, in the covering letter or executive summary. There is a fine line here between repetition and reinforcement; one of the roles of the editor is to ensure you that you remain on the right side of it.

Abstraction

Writing which is too abstract – that is to say, 'separated from matter, practice or particular examples' – is a near universal problem with proposal documents. Given that you are usually working with limited information, it is perhaps understandable if you choose to hedge your bets and avoid being too specific. But this will not help to convince the prospective client that you know how to approach the assignment or can help to tackle the issues. It is much better to present a clear and concrete vision of the way forward – while pointing out that it has been formulated on the basis of incomplete information – than merely to say 'we will be more precise once we know more about your organisation'.

The following statements are all highly abstract in nature – none helps to paint a picture of how you will get to grips with the client's problems:

> We will work with you to find suitable solutions to the issues you have raised

> This is a complex task, and we will draw upon specialists in a number of fields to devise appropriate approaches

> We are large enough to ensure that we can provide any support you may need, but small enough to give a personal service.

Avoid generalised statements which could apply to any client. Try to give concrete illustrations of how your approach or ideas might work in practice; if there is some doubt about how a particular issue should be addressed, describe the pros and cons of each option available and then *give your view on which is best*. Even if it turns out you are wrong, you will score highly for imagination and initiative provided the logic behind your answer is sound.

Self-nullification

This is usually the product of either: uncertainty or incoherence about the substance of what is being expressed; a deliberate attempt to fudge a difficult issue; or, more simply, bad drafting. The effect on the reader is however the same. By definition it creates confusion, forces the reader to guess at the writer's intentions, and will eventually undermine his or her confidence in the proposal.

Consider the following statements:

Subject to their availability, you will have unrestricted access to members of the team

Fees will not rise after the first year, unless circumstances dictate that it is necessary to review them.

We will ensure that there is a high degree of continuity in the composition of the team, although you will understand that this is not something which we are able to guarantee.

These all look like classical fudges: either the team cannot agree precisely what it should be offering or the writer is trying to have his cake and eat it. Alternatively, the team's intentions were clear but they have become mangled in the process of expression. One thing is certain: these statements would have been better left unsaid. The reader will feel let down by half-promises qualified into meaninglessness.

While the examples above look too obviously flawed to be representative, errors of this kind are surprisingly common. Watch out for them.

Ambiguity

Though more subtle than self-nullification, this problem usually has the same roots. Statements which are susceptible to more than one interpretation occur most frequently as a result of the team failing to agree explicitly about its approach.

The unsupported statement

In their enthusiasm to communicate what they believe are the team's strong points, proposal writers frequently fall into the trap of making statements which they cannot justify:

> We are well known for providing constructive, practical advice to our clients based on the highest calibre expertise.

Apart from the fact that the statement cannot be proved one way or the other, it patronises the decision-makers by implying that they are incapable of drawing their own conclusions about this team's ability to do the job. Imagine a beauty contest – the traditional sort – where contestants were assessed on how attractive *they* thought they were! Of course, the assessment is a matter for the judges, not the contestants; in the same way, do not presume on the role of the decision makers by saying how marvellous you believe yourselves to be. Instead, concentrate on *demonstrating* your strengths through the quality of thinking you apply to the prospective client's problems.

Trumpet blowing will do worse than irritate the prospective client: it will undermine his trust in you. If you cannot substantiate your claims, the decision-makers will assume that these statements are being made because you want the work, not because they are true; after all, you haven't provided any evidence which would enable them to come to any other conclusion. And without the decision-makers' trust, you stand virtually no chance of being appointed.

Take care, therefore, to avoid value judgements, and be meticulous in substantiating the qualities and attributes you will bring to the assignment.

Style

As we said earlier, the hallmark of poor style is that it obscures the transparency of the message being conveyed; the aesthetic aspects of style are a secondary consideration. Not everyone who is required at some stage in their careers to produce a proposal document will be naturally good writers; even those who are will have to work hard to make the most of their talent. But as most manifestations of poor style are caused by either confused thinking, insufficient application or weak editing, there is no excuse for failing to eradicate the weaknesses.

Jargon

Any critique of modern business communications is likely to give prominence to jargon – everyone knows what it is and nobody professes to like it. But apart from being defined as 'barbarous or debased language', it is also 'a mode of speech familiar to a group or profession'. And this is where the problem starts.

Consciously or unconsciously, people have always used jargon to promote the exclusivity – and therefore value – of their skills, expertise or professional stature. At least some of the time, this used to have the desired effect; those who were not familiar with the secret language would be suitably deferential, while those who knew it would immediately recognise one of their own. In a consumerist age, however, language designed to exclude the majority is no longer tolerated to anything like the same extent. Hence the drive by government agencies (and some private companies) to simplify forms and other types of written communication intended for use by the public.

Attitudes have similarly changed in the business-to-business context. If you are selling a technical or professional skill, the use of jargon is sure to irritate any of the decision makers whose backgrounds are different from your own. In particular, do not use technical language in proposals for smaller companies, where the decision makers are likely to be generalists with little or no grounding in your discipline. At the other end of the scale, chief executives or other senior directors of major companies may construe reliance on jargon as evidence that your firm is preoccupied with technical detail and unable to grasp the strategic objectives or implications of the assignment.

Apologists for the use of jargon will argue, however, that they are often writing on a technical subject for a technical readership, and therefore a specialised vocabulary is indispensable. In these circumstances the use of technical terms is probably unavoidable to some extent, but keep them to an absolute minimum; use Standard English alternatives wherever you can, and always ensure that the *logic* of your argument, if not some of the language in which it is couched, is transparent to the lay reader.

Excessive use of the passive voice

A stylistic curiosity is the frequency with which the passive voice is used in proposal writing. The following examples are typical:

Effective financial planning will ensure that full benefit can be taken of any opportunities to save tax.

A full review of the business will be conducted, and major issues identified and discussed.

Why not: 'effective financial planning will ensure that you benefit . . .'; and: 'we will conduct a full review of the business . . .'? The writer seems to be making an attempt to qualify his assertions by expressing them in an indirect form. The effect of this kind of phrasing is to distance the writer from the activities he is proposing and their intended effects. Prolonged use of the passive voice will leave the reader with the impression that either the firm is not wholly committed to its own recommendations, or it has some doubt about whether it can carry them out. This is hardly likely to engender trust or confidence.

Incidentally, do not try to avoid the passive voice altogether – an uninterrupted series of direct statements expressed in active mode soon becomes tiresome to read. Limited but judicious use of the passive voice will introduce an element of variety into sentence construction.

Impersonal modes of expression

Excessive use of the passive voice is often accompanied by the choice of impersonal forms of expression. Rather than referring to the name of the organisation for which the proposal has been prepared, the writer will instead allude to 'the client' – inadvertently implying that the document could have been written for *any* client:

> Once the initial appraisal has been completed, we will go through the various options with the client to ascertain the best way forward.

A proposal document is a personal statement from the team to the decision makers, and should be written as such. Ensure that you address the reader directly; intersperse the text with references to the target organisation, and use personal pronouns often.

If you need to include passages which contain technical or abstruse material, illustrate why this is relevant to the prospective client and increase the use of personal and direct forms of speech.

Verbosity

Verbosity is to the proposal writer what rising overheads are to the finance director, or inflation is to the Chancellor: an insidious enemy which can only be defeated by constant vigilance. Take the example below:

> We as a team can make a significant contribution to supporting you as you endeavour to achieve your corporate objectives. Our skills in the areas of media relations, corporate identity and graphic design, and in developing tailored communications programmes, can not only be used to promote the financial products under discussion but also to enhance your image within the UK investment community.

This passage, though rather ungainly, contains no grammatical errors and is of a standard which would be acceptable to many proposal writers and teams. It is not a particularly egregious example of verbosity. Yet what meaning would be lost if it were rewritten thus:

Our skills in media relations, corporate identity, design and other communications disciplines can also be enlisted to promote your image in the City.

Part of the editor's role is to cast a ruthless eye over the text and to simplify and shorten it wherever possible: there are always plenty of opportunities to do so.

Tautology

Tautology, the needless repetition of an idea, statement or word, crops up frequently in proposal documents: it is a pure drafting error, usually to be found in text which has been written too hastily.

> One of the main constraints on growth for European companies is their inability to expand in the current economic climate

> The effectiveness of your systems will have a bearing on the speed and efficiency with which you are able to process information

> Consecutive parts of the project will be agreed according to an agreed sequence.

These are examples where the same thing is said twice using different words, although literal repetition of adjectives and phrases is also common. As a general rule, avoid repeating the same word in a sentence unless it the definite or indefinite article, a conjunction or preposition.

Inconsistency

If more than one person has been involved in writing the document and no clear editorial direction is being exerted, stylistic inconsistencies are inevitable. It will be obvious to the reader, for example, that the following two sentences are unlikely to have been penned by the same author:

> We'd like the chance to talk over these points with you face to face.

We believe there is considerable merit in establishing a forum in which issues of this nature can be discussed informally.

Yet stylistic disparities of this enormity are often to be found within pages of each other.

In order to avoid an endlessly recurring debate about consistency in the treatment of capital letters, abbreviations, foreign words and phrases, numbers and so on, get your firm to produce a manual which sets out a recommended house style.

Condescension/presumption

These solecisms are committed most often perhaps by the traditional professions. Avoid phrases such as 'we will need to satisfy ourselves as to the reliability of your systems'. As we said in the context of 'The unsupported statement', do not presume on the decision-makers' judgement about which firm is best for their needs:

> You will find that our firm is able to offer a first class service and is ideally suited to an organisation such as yours.

The reader will not relish being patronised, even if you are a renowned expert in your field. Language of this kind will only serve to alienate and irritate.

Excessive use of bullet points

If there is one principle of proposal writing which seems to be almost universally accepted, it is that short sentences are preferable to long ones. Often they are. But a succession of abrupt, dislocated statements are as difficult to absorb as a dense block of text. To put forward a persuasive argument, words need to flow as well as ideas. Bullet points are an excellent means of summarising your material, but there is no substitute for continuous prose when attempting to convince the reader of the logic of your case.

So, these are some of the points to bear in mind if you are

charged with the onerous responsibility of writing – or reviewing – the proposal document; although we have hardly touched on grammar, syntax or the other fundamentals of language, and these are equally important. Using this section as a checklist should help to ensure that the quality of the text does not fall below an acceptable standard.

A 'MODEL' STRUCTURE

If you recognise the dangers of using boilerplate, you will treat the notion that there can be such a thing as a 'model' document with great scepticism. As we have explained, the subject matter and the way in which it is expressed cannot be determined in isolation from the circumstances of each individual tender. There is, however, similarity between the *categories* of information that need to be included in proposal documents; and there are some general principles that can be applied to the *order* in which they should be covered. These principles will provide a foundation from which you can begin to develop your synopsis.

Most documents should comprise the following elements:

- covering letter and/or executive summary
- how the objectives of the assignment will be met
- details of the team
- how the assignment will be managed
- fees
- background on the firm.

Covering letter/executive summary

Most proposers recognise the value of having a section at the beginning of the document which highlights the key messages. This can take one of several forms. The most common approach is to include an executive summary. This is usually a microcosm of the whole proposal, comprising a precis of each section. Alternatively, you might insert a page entitled 'key points' – a series of bullet points intended to emphasise the benefits of the firm's approach. Or you can incorporate this material into a covering letter.

In fact, the covering letter is one of the most under-exploited weapons in the proposer's armoury. Often it is treated as a pure formality; a two-line missive beginning with the words: 'Please find enclosed . . .'. But to overlook the potential value of the letter thus is to miss a major opportunity.

As it is the first thing which the reader sees – and may be the only part of the document which will be read thoroughly – it must have impact. A successful letter will convey your key selling points and differentiators, and catch the interest and attention of the reader. It will encourage him to read on. One way to do this is to allude to a key benefit developed in detail in a later section.

Unlike in a formal summary, you are under no obligation in the covering letter to re-present the material in the rest of the document in condensed form; you have the flexibility to introduce new material and to structure it as you choose. The letter also allows you to address the reader in a more personal way than might be deemed suitable in the body of the text; it is a good medium through which to express the 'softer' messages – for example, how important the assignment would be to your firm and the enthusiasm and commitment your team will bring to the task.

In general, it is better to have the letter bound into the document; this increases the likelihood that all the decision makers will get to see it, as well as the addressee. Also, you want to reinforce the message that the letter is an integral part of your submission.

While the letter should contain sufficient substance to engage the reader's attention, try to keep it short; two pages is usually a sensible maximum. As with any form of summary, it should be written only after the remainder of the document has been completed.

Meeting objectives

You have used the letter to capture the interest of the reader and to set the tone of the proposal; now we come to the section which usually has the greatest potential to influence the decision makers. This is your opportunity to demonstrate that you are not merely selling a set of skills or services, but have thought through how these can be applied most effectively in the light of the prospective client's particular circumstances and needs. Your best, most creative ideas belong to this section; describe the ways in which the organisation will gain from your proposals, and endeavour to link the work you will be carrying out with what you perceive are its major concerns or preoccupations.

The subject matter will, of course, depend entirely on the nature of the tender, on the prospective client and on the services you are selling. The heading could be 'Meeting your needs'; or 'The issues facing ABC Ltd.'; or 'Our response to your brief'. The possibilities are endless. Typically, however, the section will outline the substance of your proposals, and at the same time demonstrate:

- your understanding of the role of the assignment and how it will meet the organisation's objectives
- your understanding of the business and the industry in which it operates; how this understanding will contribute to the assignment
- that your proposals have been tailored to the particular needs of the business
- that you have the ability to solve problems – preferably by describing how certain issues facing the organisation should be tackled
- the benefits of your approach.

Of course, they key word here is *demonstrate*; it is not enough to say 'we are adept at solving problems' or 'our approach will bring considerable benefits'; indeed, as we suggested in our critique of *The unsupported statement*, it is much better if you don't. Describe the solutions or benefits. If you are unsure of your ground or do not have enough information to be precise, at least try to illustrate what you mean through examples of *possible* solutions or benefits.

Most people would agree that the best way of developing any

kind of relationship is (at least initially) to talk about and take an interest in the other party, not bang on about themselves. The same applies to the proposal document. In this vitally important opening section, keep references to your own firm to a minimum; its purpose is to address the issues facing the target organisation, not to discuss your own attributes.

Remember, also, that this is the place where you should be conveying ideas; avoid lapsing into prosaic descriptions of the procedures you will adopt to carry out the assignment. They will sound as if they could have been written for any client and – unless you are sure that your approach is unique in this respect – they will not help to distinguish your proposal from those of your competitors. If it is essential that this material is covered, do so in a later section.

The team

Having focused on the potential client in the first section, you should now turn the reader's attention to the resources you will bring to the assignment. The people who will actually be working with the client are of much more importance to the decision makers than the firm's overall resources and credentials; so the second section should be devoted exclusively to a description of the team.

Write a paragraph on each team member, taking care to describe both their prospective role on the assignment and why they are qualified for the job. Keep these brief: four or five lines each will usually suffice. As far as describing qualifications is concerned, details of experience with similar clients or on similar assignments is likely to be considered more relevant than paper qualifications or management roles within the firm.

If it is the type of assignment which requires a cast of thousands, it is usually better to refer only to the team leader and his or her colleagues who will have a key role on the assignment. Descriptions of more junior team members can be relegated to an appendix.

Managing the assignment

Having described the key team members and their proposed roles, it is logical to cover management issues next. These might include:

- team structure, and how it is intended to fit with the prospective client's organisation
- reporting and communications procedures, both within the team and between the team and the client
- arrangements for effecting the change-over of advisers
- the length of time it is expected that team members will work with the client (illustrate with reference to other clients where appropriate)
- quality control/customer satisfaction procedures.

This may also be the place to describe the drier aspects of the assignment, such as the technical methodologies you intend to employ.

This section will offer less opportunities for differentiation and the material will tend to be less specific than those which precede it. If, however, it does contain a key selling point – perhaps you have come up with a novel way to reduce disruption to the client's management team if you are appointed, or believe that you will be able to offer greater continuity than some of your competitors – ensure that this message is also incorporated into the covering letter or summary.

Fees

The fee section is really an extension of 'managing the assignment'. Treat it as an opportunity to convey positive messages about your commitment to giving value for money and how you intend to help the client monitor and control costs; try to show that you want the service to be as cost effective as possible, for example by showing differential billing rates and describing the distribution of senior and junior time that will be deployed on the assignment.

Apart from giving the fee itself, describe also the basis of charging and, if it is a long-term assignment, how fee levels might be determined in the future or when it would be appropriate to review them. If a detailed fee analysis is required, this may be better dealt with in an appendix.

Background on the firm

The reason for putting this last is that the material does not relate specifically to the assignment. This does not mean, however, that it can't be tailored to the reader. For example, descriptions of relevant industry experience should come before general narrative on the firm (number of offices and staff, client list etc). If possible, include short case studies, illustrating how you have tackled similar assignments.

The elements described above are not intended necessarily to correspond to chapter headings: in some cases, more headings will be required, just as you may need to discuss topics which aren't covered here. It is surprising, however, how often this broad structure can be used to good effect – across a wide range of business sectors and for diverse types of tenders.

AFTER YOU HAVE SENT THE DOCUMENT . . .

Keep in touch with the potential client; try to gauge his or her reaction to what you have written. There may be points which need to be followed up, or where the recipient requires clarification or further information. Respond with alacrity to such requests: it may help to consolidate your position. You may also be able to pick up some useful signals on which issues you should concentrate on in the presentation – or even on whether you need to refocus your approach. This can be a critical stage in the process: so do not lose any opportunity to tune into the decision-makers' thinking.

KEY POINTS

- Drafting the document is no more important than every other stage of the process – do not allow yourself to be subsumed by the task.

- Length, prose style and appearance should reflect the dispositions of the decision-makers.

- Bad style stems from a lack of clarity, which in turn implies weakness in your proposal; the quality of English will therefore have a critical (if subliminal) influence on the reader.

- Before drafting, produce a detailed synopsis and make sure it covers the objectives of the assignment, how you intend to meet them, who will do the work, how the project will be managed, what your services will cost and why your firm is qualified to perform the job.

- Whatever the production schedule, allow sufficient time for document review and proofing.

- Assign editorship of the document to one person, and never permit individual team members to alter the text in isolation from the editor; this will avoid repetition, contradiction, and inconsistency in style and content.

- Never plagiarise a past proposal; all your material needs to be tailored to the specific objectives and requirements of the prospective client.

- Focus on the organisation, not your own firm, and convey the benefits that you can offer; the document must help to convince the organisation that it will gain advantage from your appointment.

- Don't regurgitate what the target already knows or has told you at site visits; interpret the data and research findings to support your approach.

- In either writing or reviewing the document, watch out for weaknesses in style and content; common problems include jargon, the use of unsupported statements, repetition and tautology, inconsistency, verbosity and excessive use of the passive voice.

- Always include a covering letter or executive summary which conveys your key selling points and differentiators.

9

THE PRESENTATION

OBJECTIVES OF THE PRESENTATION

Leaving aside notification of the outcome, the presentation is usually the last formal stage of the proposal process; the prospective client will be conscious that the assessments he or she has been making of the competing firms up to that point will shortly need to be translated into a final decision. Perhaps for this reason, many proposers regard the presentation as the only critical phase, and all the others as mere formalities. Of course, such a blinkered view can only diminish a proposal team's chances of succeeding. Yet it is undeniable that in practice the result often does hang on the team's performance at the presentation, particularly if the decision-makers feel that there is little to choose between the contenders.

A formal presentation, or at least a meeting, is a stipulated requirement in the vast majority of competitive tenders. Seen from the decision-makers' perspective, the presentation fulfils a number of functions which the document cannot. For example, it is likely to provide:

Insight into the personalities of the team members and the culture of the firm they represent

Consciously or unconsciously, the decision-makers will treat the presentation as a simulation of what the team will be like to work with. It will shed light on a number of crucial questions: does the team act *as* a team, or as a group of seemingly unrelated individuals? Is it consensus-orientated, or dominated by one person? Do the team members appear to have clearly defined roles? Is their manner confident or defensive? Do we feel that we can *trust* them? Similarly, the presentation will give some indication of the firm's style: whether, for example, it is old-fashioned or progressive, egalitarian or autocratic, formal or relaxed and so on. The inferences drawn in these areas will influence the decision-makers' judgement of how the team is likely to behave and perform on the assignment. That judgement is bound to weigh heavily in their deliberations.

Equally important, the presentation will give an indication of how the team reacts under pressure. Even if the meeting is relaxed and informal, the contenders will not be able to forget that a great deal is riding on their performance, and that any mistakes at this stage are likely to be irrevocable. This will also help the decision-makers to form a view on whether they feel they can trust them, and how they are likely to respond if problems arise during the course of the assignment.

Insight into the team's commitment to the assignment

The decision-makers will already have gained an impression of the proposers' level of interest and enthusiasm for the assignment from the quality of the document, but a much more concrete indication of their attitude will be provided by the face-to-face encounter. However, the decision-makers will be looking for more than an ebullient manner (indeed, that might even put them off); the quality and rigour of thought which the team has put into its proposals, the extent to which the team members have understood the organisation and its activities, their eagerness to find solutions and to be helpful in any way they can – these are the characteristics which the prospective client will not fail to notice and take into account.

An indication of team members' technical skills and competence

As the process of drafting and producing the document is invisible to the decision-makers, it is hard for them on this evidence alone to judge the technical skills, intelligence and sagacity of individual team members. At the presentation, however, team members will be required to give spontaneous responses to decision-makers' questions; the prospective client will not have a better opportunity to assess their abilities. This underlines the crucial role of the question-and-answer part of the meeting; the team's performance at this stage is more likely to influence the outcome than their formal presentation.

An opportunity to clarify points discussed in the document and probe for weaknesses

The question-and-answer session also gives the decision-makers the chance to cross-examine the team on areas where it might be vulnerable. Of course, they will have expected the document to have portrayed the team's experience, expertise and track record in the best possible light; the presentation gives an opportunity to scrutinise these claims in more detail and to ascertain whether the team is able successfully to defend them. The presentation will also give an indication of the team's attitude to their proposed fee, and whether the team leader is prepared to negotiate a reduction.

A tie-break where the decision is close

As mentioned above, the presentation is likely to assume greater importance if two or more of the competing firms have performed equally well during the preceding stages. If there is still no appreciable difference after the presentation, and the proposed fees are the same, intangible qualities such as personal chemistry are likely to prevail; the decision-makers will be asking themselves with which team they were able to establish the best rapport. Remember, it is wrong to assume that 'chemistry' need be a mystical phenomenon which is beyond proposers' control. The team which looks the decision-makers in the eye, addresses their questions directly, is able to depart from their prepared course if a new issue is raised, and has the sensitivity to distinguish concerns which are of critical importance from those which are marginal, are likely to achieve a rapport with their interlocutors – whether they are aware of it or not.

Of course, from the proposer's standpoint, the presentation has a different set of objectives. In addition to making a favourable impression in the areas referred to above, they may include: to reinforce the key messages in the document; to emphasise the benefits of the team's approach; and possibly to clarify any points where there is room for misunderstanding or which have yet to be resolved. This raises the question of the relationship between the oral and written exercises, and how the subject matter of the proposal should be distributed between the two.

Some proposers use the presentation merely to recapitulate the main points in the document, often because they suspect that one or more of the decision makers hasn't read it. The trouble with this approach is that it is likely to disappoint (or even insult) the listener if he has. The presentation will have much greater impact if you either introduce entirely fresh material or develop some of the points in the document in greater detail.

The introduction of new material can be highly effective, especially if it is in some way topical. One possibility is to give a commentary on a recent development affecting the prospective client's business – one, perhaps, which has occurred between the submission of the document and the date of the presentation. Similarly, a point you have developed on paper can be given extra force if at the oral you develop a new angle or provide additional material with which to corroborate it.

The presentation can also be used to convey information or messages which for some reason are unsuitable for inclusion in the document. As a one-way form of communication, the document affords no opportunity to gauge the reaction of the reader or to respond if any objections are raised. It may therefore be unwise to use the written medium to raise issues which are likely to be highly sensitive or controversial. This does not mean that the document should be bland; only that some matters are better dealt with face-to-face.

For example: while it is always a bad idea overtly to knock the competition, you may feel that the prospective client should be aware of certain differences between your position and that of another contender. Assuming that you feel it is appropriate to raise this at all, it will almost certainly be better to discuss it over the boardroom table than in writing. Let's say that during the course of the proposal, you have been asked to comment on the performance of one of the organisation's departments. You form the opinion that the department is not functioning effectively and staff changes are needed. This could well be a situation where the prospective client will not appreciate your committing your ideas to paper: use the greater confidentiality of the presentation instead.

Deciding which points to include in the document and which to raise at the presentation should form part of your team discussions on strategy. Once the document is out the way, preparation for the oral becomes your top priority.

PREPARATION

Of course, some people are naturally more effective presenters than others. Consequently, it is a popularly held view that it is better to not let some individuals anywhere near a presentation while others should do more than their fair share. This view is flawed for a number of reasons, not least of which is the fact that there are seldom enough really strong presenters to go round. But whatever the presenters' innate attributes, the key to consistently high performance is thorough preparation. It is a mistake to assume that good speakers can afford to skimp on this phase. Those who do will be seen for what they are: talented communicators who have not fully mastered their subject, or spent enough time thinking through the issues and anticipating the prospective client's questions or concerns.

Reconnaissance

Your preparations should encompass the circumstances of the presentation, as well as the presentation itself. Some basic research should provide useful pointers in planning and developing your approach.

First, find out who from the organisation will be in attendance: this may affect the emphasis you give to the presentation, or even who you decide to field from your side. Consider also how many people will be present. As a rule of thumb, your team should not outnumber the representatives from the prospective client.

Most presentations are conducted at the clients' premises. If possible, arrange a visit in advance so that you can assess the venue. What are the physical properties of the room in which the presentation is to be held, and how might this affect the way you conduct the meeting? Consider, for example, the likely positions in which your team and the panel will be sitting; the lighting and acoustics; and whether there are facilities for using visual aids. If you and your competitors are due to present on the same day, it can be helpful to know who is scheduled to appear before and after you, particularly if you have a good idea of the approaches other firms are likely to take: it will focus your attention on creating impact and differentiation.

While most prospective clients will leave it to you to decide how the meeting should be conducted it is as well to know whether they have any fixed preconceptions: for example, are they expecting an informal discussion or a highly structured, 'theatrical' presentation? The decision-makers' expectations should not necessarily deflect you from your preferred course; but you should at least be aware of them. If you have opted for an approach which may surprise the audience, you will need to show that you are conscious of the fact – perhaps through your introduction.

Developing the material

We have said that you should use the presentation to do more than merely recapitulate the main points in the document, and that it can be helpful to pick up on topical issues or to develop fresh angles. But how do you decide what material should go in, and what should be left out?

If the strategy meeting which preceded the drafting of the document were effective, this ground will already have been covered to some extent. You will have in mind some particularly strong points which you intend to include in the presentation. Now you need to develop these further. Return to the issues, features and benefits matrix and, in discussion with the proposal team, try to refine it. Build into your deliberations any new information which has come to light; consider in particular:

- external events which may have an impact on the prospective client's business, or which might affect the proposal itself
- feedback on the document; if you have had the opportunity to discuss your submission with the recipient or any of the decision-makers, consider the parts they said they liked, or those which they seem to regard as being particularly important. While natural reticence may have deterred them from spelling out the parts they *didn't* like, you should be able to identify any ideas or themes to which they are perhaps less receptive from their general manner and tone
- the team's perceptions of the key issues and your side's major selling points, and whether these have changed since the submission of the document
- anything that is known about your competitors, and the approach they may have taken to the proposal process as a whole and are likely to take specifically to the presentation.

From this discussion you should be able to decide the thrust of what you want to say.

In considering the type of subject matter you should include and emphasise in the presentation, remember the principles you applied to the document: they are even more relevant here. Above all, demonstrate that you have understood the prospective client's business and that the approaches and solutions you are offering are tailored accordingly. If you fail to do this, be prepared for reactions ranging from indifference to downright indignation. Here is an example that falls into the latter end of the spectrum:

> When we were thinking of going public, we had a number of present-ations from bankers and brokers. They were appalling, and the people were largely clueless. They had totally failed to do the fundamental thing, and put themselves in the position of the audience. They droned on for ages about their company, and made a few noises about us based on absolutely no knowledge at all – one of them even said 'we don't know anything about your industry, but we're sure it's a very interest-ing sector'. The firm we eventually appointed won largely because they'd included our logo on their slides – at least they had acknow-ledged us, and it conveyed a sense of our working together. Our overall impression of the process was they were all bright people, but hopeless at convincing us that they were right for the job.

The amount of time you devote to your own firm and its track record should be strictly limited. Make sure, even when you do refer to the attributes of the team or your firm, that these are closely linked with the prospective client's objectives and requirements. The same applies when you are demonstrating your technical command of your subject. The audience will listen if you tell them something they don't already know; but the way to seize their attention is to put that knowledge into a relevant context. According to one chartered surveyor:

> What really matters is market knowledge – and that means being as up to date as possible. Potential clients are turned on if, during a present-ation, you can peel off historical knowledge about similar projects, letting details, prices per square foot etc, and we use this to extrapolate a solution or approach to their particular requirements. Demon-strating that you know your market is critical, and they love it when you use that knowledge to give them the answer they're looking for.

One of the critical differences between the document and the presentation, however, is the number of points it is safe to raise. In the document you can aim for comprehensiveness – anything which is relevant or material to your case can be included. In the presentation, by contrast, you must remember that the listeners' capacity to absorb information has its limits. If you attempt to bombard them with too many messages – even though each may comprise a major benefit of clear importance to the audience – you risk two unfortunate consequences. The first is that during the presentation, you will fail to hold the listeners' attention. The second is that afterwards, at the point at which decisions are being made, they may find it difficult to recall *anything* that you said. It is difficult to generalise, but you should aim to shape your material into perhaps three key points, expressed as benefits to the decision-makers. All the other points you want to make should then be enlisted to support these key assertions. This doesn't mean that you shouldn't go into detail in the presentation; only that the use of detail must be highly selective. As one experienced proposer puts it:

> In the past, we have made the mistake of over presenting – giving far too much information: too many credentials and too many solutions. We now try to be much more specific on one or two key areas, which means fewer ideas but more analysis of the problem.

Structure

The need to create a 'hierarchy' of material, in which layers of sub-points are built up to corroborate a major conclusion, means that structure is all-important. The development of structure is best approached in a series of stages.

First, make a note of all the points which you think could be relevant. Pay no attention to their respective importance – the only objective at this stage is to capture all the ideas and thoughts which might have a role to play in your presentation. Second, begin to group points which are related to each other, perhaps discarding any which are marginal to your case along the way. Third, distinguish between key points and supporting points in each category.

Remember, key points should express an advantage or benefit to the prospective client.

This is the 'bottom-up' approach; you have analysed all the material at your disposal and assembled it to reach some fundamental conclusions. Now adopt a 'top-down' approach. Try to think of a unitary theme which binds all your material together: it might, for example, encapsulate the essence of what you believe the decision makers need to achieve their objectives. Then construct the key points which convey how you intend to contribute to the delivery of these objectives; then think about the supporting material and illustrations you need to demonstrate that you are able to make this contribution. The 'top-down' and bottom-up' approaches should provide the same answer. If they don't, you may be thinking of the wrong examples to support the main thrust of your case, or alternatively the overall theme of the presentation may not fit in with what you are actually able to offer. In this case, you will need to think through the material again. In due course, you should arrive at a structure which can be described graphically in the following terms:

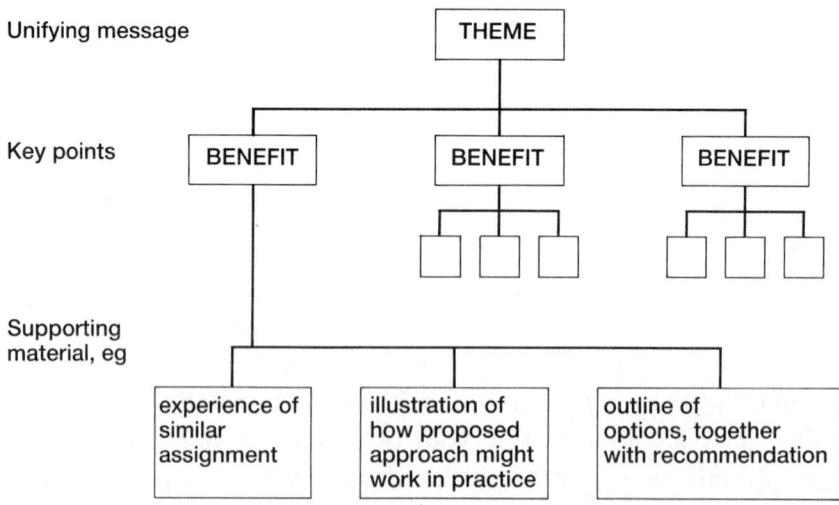

Figure 9.1   'Vertical' structure of presentation material

The subject matter of the key points and supporting material will, of course, depend entirely on the nature of what you are selling and to whom; but the principle of subdividing the contents in the manner described will hold good in nearly all circumstances.

You will also need to consider the 'horizontal' structure of the presentation; that is to say, the beginning, middle and end. The famous public speaking maxim of 'tell them what you're going to say, say it, and tell what you've said' is a useful guide; although if there is more than one presenter you should not interpret this too literally, or you run the risk that the presentation will sound rather mechanistic.

Even if the presentation team is large, you must try to find a formal speaking part for each member. It is risky to take along a 'technician' exclusively to answer questions on the more esoteric aspects of the assignment; the anticipated questions may not be raised and, in any case, the panel is likely to feel uncomfortable with a team member who appears to have a minor or poorly defined function. Remember everything that was said in Chapter 4 about definition of roles and their importance to the prospective client.

Introduce some variations between the structures of the individual presentations. The team leader, for example, can be used to set the scene and summarise the key points at the end, without

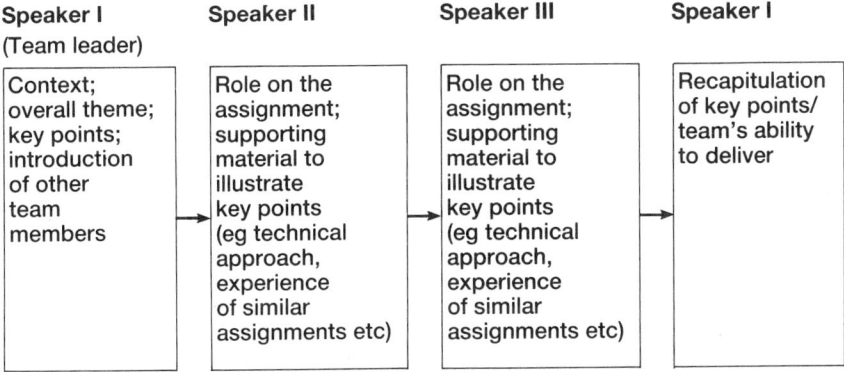

Speaker I (Team leader)	Speaker II	Speaker III	Speaker I
Context; overall theme; key points; introduction of other team members	Role on the assignment; supporting material to illustrate key points (eg technical approach, experience of similar assignments etc)	Role on the assignment; supporting material to illustrate key points (eg technical approach, experience of similar assignments etc)	Recapitulation of key points/ team's ability to deliver

Figure 9.2   'Horizontal' structure of the presentation

touching on any technical detail, while the other members may concentrate on conveying supporting material to underpin the key points. For a three member team, the horizontal structure of the presentation might resemble Fig. 9.2.

At the stage where you are ready to develop the raw material for the presentation, each team member should create a vertical structure for their own contribution, deciding which points should be used to support which. Then, as a group, the individual contributions will be welded together to form a horizontal structure for the presentation as a whole. The overall effect of a well-structured presentation is not that the audience will necessarily remember everything that you said; but that they will remember the key messages – and that these were well supported and cogently argued.

Style and format

As with the document, the style and format of the presentation should take account of the culture of the organisation to whom you are proposing and the attitudes and predispositions of the decision-makers. There are, however, some general principles which should be borne in mind.

Some presentations – those, for example, given by management consultants at the end of a substantial project – may (justifiably) last for hours. But the *new business presentation* is an idiom apart – convincing your audience to hire you for an assignment is fundamentally different from giving a seminar, speaking at a conference or reporting back on work already completed. For one thing, in a competitive tender the audience will have to listen to a number of presentations covering much the same ground as your own – worse still, all the presentations may be held on the same day, or indeed afternoon. This is a good reason for keeping your presentation short. The decision-makers are likely to appreciate the fact that you have tried to condense your material; some may even take the view that the team which cannot put its message across within a reasonable time frame may prove to be extravagant with the precious commodity when it comes to the job itself:

> We [a US financial services company] are either asked to make a presentation by lawyers or accountants wanting to know how we can help their clients, or by company directors interested in corporate services. In both cases, I take no more than 15 minutes, even if they're prepared to sit there for longer (in which case I'll make a feature of it). In fact it's usually a bad sign if they're prepared to let you drone on. I work on the basis that if you can't get over the key points in a quarter of an hour you shouldn't have bothered them in the first place. Time is money, and people really believe that here.

The amount of time you take over your presentation will vary according to the circumstances; there are plenty of occasions where 15 minutes might even be considered perfunctory, or abrupt. But, as a rule of thumb, aim to complete it within half an hour. If the prospective client allocates you a longer period – which will often be the case – suggest that the remaining time is devoted to questions and informal exchanges on what you have presented.

Perhaps the most important principle of all about presentations for new work is that, as far as possible, they should be treated as ordinary business meetings. Remember the distinction between *qualification* and *selection* in the buying process; by the time you reach the presentation stage, the prospective client is likely to have formed a clear view of your credentials and capabilities, and will be much more interested in what you will be like to work with. Treating a new business presentation with the informality you would normally associate with an ordinary meeting will help the decision-makers to picture what you will be like to work with; it will give them a foretaste of how you will conduct the assignment and how the relationship is likely to develop. All this will help you to engender the trust and confidence they must feel to award you the job. An excessively formal approach to the presentation may indeed disappoint the decision-makers, particularly if you have already begun to establish a close relationship:

> In one case, we had taken part in a series of exploratory meetings where we worked closely with the marketing director. I made the

mistake of putting on a large-scale presentation with four or five people, which we lost. The marketing director told me he'd really enjoyed the first stages, but had been turned off by the rather robotic presentation.

If you accept the logic of this argument, you should also be sceptical about the value of visual aids – unless used judiciously, they can have the effect of putting a barrier between you and the decision makers and increasing the stiffness of the occasion.

Visual aids range from simple flipcharts and 'storyboards' through to 35mm slides, overhead projector acetates, video and various forms of TV-style graphics where a monitor is used. Probably the most common, and potentially the most dangerous, are the 35mm slides. Dangerous? Think about what happens when this medium is employed. First, the room has to be darkened in order to see the images clearly – thus casting the presenter into obscurity and reducing eye contact between the team and the decision-makers. Second, the presenter has the whirr of the machine to contend with – a distraction at the best of times. Third, 35mm slides commit the presenter to a pre-determined course: the order of the slides cannot be changed once the presentation has started and it is impossible to switch easily between formal presentation and discussion, and back again. Fourth, most important of all, the slides rather than the presenter become the focal point of the audience's attention; and finally, there is always the risk that the slides have been put into the carousel in the wrong order or that in some way they get out of sync with what the presenter is saying. According to one finance director:

> The firms which present to us always seem to depend heavily on slides. But slick presentations don't impress us at all – we are interested in the content of what they're saying not whether there are flashy graphics. Of course, it is always quite amusing when they go wrong . . .

The point is that none of these factors is likely to be conducive to building rapport with the decision-makers at the presentation, and all may create unwanted distractions which will reduce the impact of your key messages. Flipcharts and overhead slides are generally preferable because they afford you greater flexibility, but even here presenters must be careful to ensure that they themselves remain the focus of attention, and that the visual aids are no more than tools to reinforce or corroborate what they are saying.

Some presenters argue that, as visual information is easier to assimilate than the spoken word, it is helpful to use slides as a 'road map' through the presentation and to emphasis the key points. But if your material has been structured effectively, the audience will have no difficulty following the format or grasping the crucial messages. Too often, visual aids are used as a prop for the presenters rather than as a means of illuminating the audience; they make it easier for the presenters to keep to the point and maintain coherence, particularly if they are not too sure of their subject or have not spent enough time on preparation.

Visual aids are at their most effective when you need to convey information which is not easily expressed other than through graphical means – for example, a bar chart will get your message across more quickly and simply than reciting a series of statistics. There are also instances, for example in the advertising and design-related industries, where the product itself requires visual treatment or display. In both cases, the visual part of the present-ation will have a greater sense of 'drama' if it is contrasted with a conversational approach to the remainder of the presentation, rather than merely integrated into a series of slides running from beginning to end.

Another frequently used device is to produce documentation to be left behind at the end of the presentation:

> Where there's a choice, we prefer not to send a document in advance – we like to make an impact at our presentation, rather than risk getting bogged down in detailed questioning on the day because they've been through the document line by line. The document's role is to summar-ise our credentials and what we told them at the presentation.

While in most cases a document *is* required in advance, if the potential client has asked you only to attend a presentation it will usually be a good idea to prepare a leave-behind document. In these circumstances, make sure that the document is distributed at the *end* of the presentation and not the beginning – otherwise the audience will leaf their way through it while you are speaking and will be unable to recall what has been said.

If visual aids can stand in the way of good communication, it follows that having a prepared script which is either read or memorised is likely to have the same effect. The presentation is likely to go well if you can provoke reactions from your audience and generate debate; in order to do that, you must convey a sense of spontaneity and make the material sound fresh. You will find this impossible if you try to play safe and read from a script. It doesn't matter if you stumble over a few words: the important thing is that you will be reaching out to your audience, maintaining contact with them, and observing their reactions. By all means use notes, but remember not to read them and speak at the same time. Practise getting into the rhythm where you look down, decide what you are going to say, look up, engage the audience, and keep looking up until it is time to refer again to your notes; then pause, decide what you are going to say next, look up and so on. You will find that this is the best way to keep the listener's attention, while the pauses will act as essential breaks which will enable the audience to digest what you've just said.

The fact that you should treat the presentation as an ordinary business meeting doesn't mean that it can't have a theatrical quality. For example, consider starting the presentation with an arresting statement or rhetorical question; something which immediately seizes the listener's attention. Indeed, the only parts of the presentation which you should memorise in advance are the opening and closing lines: the beginning must have impact to get you off to a good start, while at the end you need a strong cadence to round off the presentation and signal finality to the listener.

Rehearsing

Always rehearse – even if you think you know your material back to front. There is an argument that too many rehearsals kill spontaneity, but in truth developing a confident, spontaneous, 'natural' style requires practice – as all the world's best public performers know.

Rehearsing is particularly important if you are fielding a multiple-member team. Not only will it help to build rapport between the team members, and familiarise presenters with each other's material; it is also an opportunity to perfect smooth hand-overs between individual presentations and decide, for example, how to handle the introductions at the beginning of the meeting.

The main purpose of rehearsing, however, is to practise your delivery of the material and to prepare for questions which the panel may put to you. In order to do this effectively, you need to get senior members of your firm who are not part of the present-ation team to form a 'panel' and simulate the role of the decision-makers. The use of this panel should, however, be approached with some caution.

The team should begin by rehearsing on its own – there is no point in introducing outsiders until the speakers are confident with their material and have decided how the individual presentations fit together. But the formal rehearsals, delivered in front of an external panel, shouldn't be left until the last moment either; there is nothing more potentially damaging to the team's confidence and equilibrium than to be bombarded with new ideas and approaches by senior colleagues just before a presentation is about to take place. Moreover, the panel should be thoroughly briefed in advance (perhaps by the proposal manager) so that its members understand the background to the proposal and why the team has chosen to tackle the presentation in the way that it has. The briefing will also help them to devise some testing questions to put to the team at the end of the dry run.

The team should use these formal rehearsals to develop the way it intends to interact with the 'real' audience on the day. Presenters should work on the rhythm of speaking and pausing, and main-taining eye contact. (Try not to let the eyes flicker between mem-bers of the audience; engage the chairman of the panel for say, six seconds, and then look at each of the panel members in turn for a similar period before returning to the chairman. In this way, each member of the panel will feel involved and included in the present-ation.) This is also a good time for team members to decide what to do when they are not speaking. It is usually best if the non-speakers alternate between looking at the speaker and members of the panel; needless to say, they should at all times be attentive. Try to prevent team members from simultaneously glaring at the chair-man – this is apt to look robotic and intimidating. There is, how-ever, no mechanical formula for how the team should interact with its audience. Try out various approaches at the rehearsals and decide which is likely to work most effectively.

The question-and-answer session which usually follows the formal part of the presentation often proves to be one of the most crucial aspects of the whole proposal process – so ensure that at least 50 per cent of your rehearsal time is devoted to it. The team should spend considerable time in the run up to the presentation trying to anticipate the questions the decision-makers are likely to ask and formulating suitable answers. In addition, the rehearsal panel should prepare questions and role-play exchanges with the team. It is important, of course, to make the questions as challenging as possible.

Rehearsing these exchanges will quickly help to identify and eradicate weaknesses. In fact, a number of these recur frequently and are worthy of a special mention. The first concerns the team leader. He or she should constrain any impulses to dominate the proceedings and instead act as chairman, referring questions to team members as appropriate; he should only answer questions himself when directed to do so by the panel, or if he is clearly the best qualified to provide a response. Leaders who attempt to handle all the questions themselves tend to undermine the apparent cohesiveness of the team and – worse – they create the impression that they have less than complete confidence in their colleagues.

Ensure that answers are direct and to the point: keep them short. Avoid the tendency to over-qualify responses, or they will ramble and you will begin to sound defensive. Do not introduce material which is irrelevant to the question.

It is common for decision-makers to raise issues relating to your fee at the presentation, and it is here that many presenters come unstuck by appearing to be indecisive. Think through what their questions are likely to be and practise your response at rehearsals. It is most important that you are able confidently to maintain a clear and unambiguous position on costs even under vigorous probing; you need to decide how you should handle any attempts to get you to reduce your fees, and how far you are willing to negotiate if some form of discount is requested. Remember what was said in Chapter 7: be prepared to defend your position over fees and be conscious that too ready a capitulation may raise doubts over your credibility.

Use the rehearsals to practise finishing the presentation on a positive note. It is likely that when the panel's questions have run their course, the chairman will ask you if there is anything you wish to add. You may have some questions of your own which you want to put to the panel; if you do, make sure they are related to major strategic issues or areas you know are of concern or interest to the decision-makers – this is not the time to raise technical details which could be sorted out after the presentation. Finally, prepare some crisp valedictory remarks, perhaps to the effect that the team has enjoyed working on the proposal and is enthusiastic about the prospect of carrying out the assignment.

ON THE DAY

Do not have a team rehearsal on the day of the presentation – it could raise questions or doubts over some aspect of your approach which you won't have time to resolve. If possible, however, try to get the team to spend some time together shortly beforehand (breakfast or lunch is a good idea). Talk over the main points and revisit the more difficult questions you are likely to be asked, and how you intend to address them. The leader should use this occasion to build the team's confidence and cohesiveness.

At the presentation itself, do not be surprised if the panel pursue a tougher line of questioning or have a more aggressive attitude than you have experienced during the proposal process up to that point; it may only mean that the decision-makers are taking your ideas seriously, and want to probe for weaknesses.

If the presentation leader intends to mention the roles or experience of his colleagues during the presentation, keep the introductions at the beginning of the meeting as brief as possible – just give their names and sit down. Some presenters like to begin by saying how long they intend to speak for, requesting that questions are taken at the end. This is a matter of personal style, although bear in mind that interruptions can be turned to your advantage: they might lead to a fruitful discussion which would otherwise not take place. It is generally a good sign if the panel actively participates in your presentation, rather than merely absorbs it.

Be prepared to change direction. If the decision-makers show a particular interest in one topic, discuss it with them fully before turning to other subjects. One of the messages you should be trying to convey at the presentation is that you are capable of listening as well as speaking.

After the presentation, get the team together to discuss how it went and whether there is a need for immediate further action: you may have agreed, for example, to provide extra information on a particular point. In a major proposal, the team is sure to have invested a great deal of time and effort on the project. So it is also a good idea to arrange a small celebration – even though you don't yet know the result.

KEY POINTS

- Don't simply recapitulate the main points in the document; the presentation will have far greater impact if you use additional material, develop new angles and expand on key themes.

- Consider using new information which has emerged since the submission of the document, relating for example to external events, what you have discovered about your competitors' approach and feedback on the document itself; above all, aim to tell your audience something they don't already know.

- Where appropriate, use the presentation to raise contentious or sensitive issues which were inappropriate for inclusion in the proposal document.

- Even good presenters must prepare and rehearse thoroughly; everyone in attendance needs to demonstrate a command of their subject and should try to anticipate the potential client's concerns and questions.

- Find out in advance who and how many will attend from the organisation; make sure your team does not outnumber theirs.

- Where possible, reconnoitre the presentation room and try to discover where you have been placed in the running order.

- Consider what style of presentation is most appropriate: for instance, formal or informal, 'theatrical' or low-key?

- Don't bombard your audience with too much information; shape your material into a few key points and express them as benefits.

- Each team member present must be given a speaking role; don't risk taking along a 'technician' who may not be able to contribute.

- Restrict your presentation to around 30 minutes; devote any remaining time to questions and answers, and informal discussion.

- Be careful how you use visual aids; they may put a barrier between you and the audience.

- Remember not to distribute documentation until the session is over.

- Debrief your team immediately afterwards and consider whether you need to supply more information.

10

FOLLOW-UP

AFTER THE PRESENTATION

The presentation might be the last formal stage of the proposal, but this doesn't mean that the process is over: the prospective client, for example, may want more information from you before taking a final decision. Then, when the result is announced, you should debrief both your own team and, preferably, the target organisation. You should also be looking for ways in which you can capitalise on any additional opportunities highlighted by the tender process, and taking appropriate action to ensure that your firm benefits from the experience.

Waiting for the result

There can often be a long gap between the presentation and being informed of the result. In exceptional cases, you may never be told at all – although in such circumstances you might reflect that any organisation which does not have the courtesy to inform you of its decision is probably not one that you would enjoy working with anyway. But the organisation will usually have given you an indication in the invitation to tender or at the presentation of when they intend to notify you of their decision. If not, ask them at the presentation.

Don't be too concerned if there is a long silence; it's not necessarily bad news. The target may be asking your competitors supplementary questions, or simply finding it difficult to come to a decision.

Using the time productively

Try to stay in touch with the decision-makers while they are making their deliberations. Don't pester them, but ask your contacts within the organisation how they think you fared at the presentation, whether you successfully conveyed the messages you intended and if there would be any advantage in clarifying some of the key points.

Where it is clear that the organisation is having difficulty in making its final choice, you might suggest to your contacts that they consider inviting each firm to do something more, such as attend a second meeting or submit some further documentation. This won't be necessary in most cases, but it may be helpful where it is apparent that the decision-makers need a tie-break. Taking the initiative in this way may itself give you the edge.

Answering additional enquiries

Of course, it could be that it is your firm from which the organisation wants more information. For example, the decision-makers may have been uncertain about your charging structure or want a more detailed breakdown of your proposed time commitment, or they may have had doubts about a particular member of your team, whom they wish you to consider replacing.

To some extent, you will have been forewarned by the signals transmitted at the presentation – such as looks of surprise or misunderstanding on the faces of the panel members. More often than not, any uncertainties will surface during the question-and-answer session; a large number of questions on an issue which you thought was clear-cut is a sure sign that you have failed to get your message across.

In instances where you are convinced that the organisation did not fully understand what you were saying (or where, for whatever reason, you missed out a key part of your proposal), you might consider writing a follow-up letter immediately after the presentation to clarify the area where you feel you have been misunderstood or to include the information which you left out. Do not do this as a matter of course, however. If it looks as though the decision-makers are quite happy with what they have been told, making a further, unsolicited approach could be counter-productive.

Most requests for additional information are likely to be made over the telephone and, in many cases, you can probably provide an answer on the spot or a few hours later. In all cases, you must respond promptly.

Sometimes the potential client may simply be unable to decide. While not very satisfactory from your point of view – you are bound to wonder whether you could have done more to reinforce the appeal of your proposition – it is common enough to find the prospective client torn between two choices.

If you are faced with this predicament, do not in the first instance merely offer to cut the fee. Suggest instead a more informal meeting to discuss the organisation's main areas of concern or – if you have to – a second presentation on the key points of your proposal. You might even suggest that the organisation gives you and your competitor the opportunity to undertake a mini-project of some sort so that the decision-makers can see both sides in action and judge from the results.

Just such a situation was encountered by a large UK public relations consultancy. The chairman explained how the impasse was resolved:

> I received an embarrassed 'phone call from the potential client after we and another agency had completed our presentations. He told me they had discussed our relative merits endlessly, but still couldn't decide which one to appoint. I responded by offering to do a second presentation, to get together with the other agency in a room and have both sides answer the same questions, and to perform a small piece of work in competition with the other consultancy. My contact called me a week later and said they'd chosen the second agency. When I asked him how they had arrived at their decision, he told me they'd done it by flipping a coin!

This is a miserable way to lose and, for the successful firm, an unsatisfactory way to win. Fortunately, however, arbitrary decisions like this do not happen very often; most buyers will go to great lengths to find a rational way to settle the outcome, so it is in your interests to suggest appropriate methods of breaking the deadlock.

Additional opportunities

You should always be alert to the possibility that the organisation may present your firm with opportunities other than the assignment which you were asked to propose for. Some may have become apparent during the course of the proposal – perhaps at the site visits, for example, when you might have been told about key issues and problems in other areas.

If you have won the tender, you should already be thinking about how, in addition to the project which you have been awarded, the client may need other services provided by your firm. If you lost, bear in mind that the organisation may have a deliberate policy of using several firms of advisers, and that they may consider employing you on a different assignment. The debriefing process, described below, can prove helpful in identifying just such opportunities.

Remember, then, that although the proposal process has finished, the relationship you have established with the organisation might still bear fruit; and that in any case it would be unwise to alienate the individuals who have decided to pass you over on this occasion – they could eventually become important clients.

DEBRIEFING

Proposers tend to be rather casual about finding out why they won – or lost. Winners perhaps see little point in pressing their new clients on this issue, while nobody likes to spend too long dwelling on failure. But given the time, money and effort that will have gone into your proposal, you should try to maximise the return on your investment by finding out what you did right and where you went wrong.

The discipline of debriefing is especially important in circumstances where your firm has won. Understandably, the first reaction is often to breathe a huge sigh of relief, congratulate everyone involved, have a cosy lunch with the new client – at which, perhaps, one or two observations may be given on how your firm performed – and leave it at that.

This somewhat half-hearted approach to debriefing is a mistake for several reasons. To begin with, it could be that you won because your competitors were untypically unimpressive on this occasion – which doesn't necessarily mean that you *were* impressive. You need to know precisely what it was that your team said or did which gave you the advantage, or whether it was something of a victory by default. The debriefing process should also give you an opportunity to discover more about your competitors; if you forego the debriefing, you might be missing out on a great deal of important intelligence – not just about how they approach tenders, but also how they structure their services, manage their resources, define their main differentiators and so on.

Another good reason for debriefing a winning proposal with the client is that it can often reveal more about what he is expecting from you – and, in particular, whether your proposal may have created a mismatch of expectations. Finding out if there is likely to be a problem in this respect even before the assignment has started puts you in a good position to carry out whatever remedial action is required to avoid dissatisfaction later on. Thus, the debriefing can be seen as the first step of a client service programme.

Remember, no proposal is perfect – even the one that wins. You must find out what you could have done better.

Was it a failure?

However artificial it may seem, try not to think of losing as a failure. In a commercial environment where competitive tendering is increasingly the norm, you have to accept that you cannot win everything. The worst response to a losing tender is for the firm's senior management to embark on a witch-hunt of those involved. This will merely discourage people in your firm from wanting to become involved in proposals in the future.

In the long term, the quality of your performance can prove to be more important than the actual result. A strong performance throughout the tender process will stand your firm in good stead the next time the project goes out to tender or, as we have already suggested, may put you first in line for additional work in a complementary area. Potential clients will not suddenly change their opinion of your firm just because you haven't won the job. As one finance director explains:

> None of the firms which got through to the second round of the tender blotted their copybook in any way – it just happened that they didn't quite achieve the winner's edge. But that doesn't mean we wouldn't consider using them for other work. Quite the opposite, in fact: the tender process proved an extremely valuable means of identifying advisers who I'm certain we will wish to work with in future.

How should you go about the task of finding out why you won or lost?

Your team

Start with your own proposal team. When you are notified of the result, bring your team members together and discuss what were likely to be the critical success factors. Does the prospective client's choice seem logical given their previously expressed priorities and requirements, or was it totally unexpected? How did they explain their decision? Were their reasons credible, or does the outcome suggest a competitor had an inside track?

This discussion is important in order to focus the external debriefing.

Who should be debriefed?

In most cases, the individual whom you should debrief will be obvious. He will probably have acted as your main point of contact throughout the proposal process and, provided he was one of the decision-makers, should be the person whose views you seek.

Sometimes, however, this individual may have been strongly influenced by someone else – either above or below in the decision-making chain. The more senior person might be the chief executive or managing director; the more junior, an assistant who had been charged with the task of summarising or comparing the key points of each firm's tender. In these cases, you may need to canvas the views of two or possibly three individuals in order to form a complete picture.

That may not be possible, of course, and you should continue to be careful about taking up too much of the organisation's time. The team leader should make the final decision on whose views are the most important and whether it is appropriate to approach more than one individual.

Debriefing options

There are essentially four options for debriefing a potential client:

(i)   a written questionnaire;
(ii) a personal interview conducted by a member of the proposal team;
(iii) a personal interview conducted by a representative of your firm who was not part of the team;
(iv) a personal interview conducted by a third party on your behalf.

A written questionnaire

Some proposers will send the organisation a multiple-choice questionnaire, asking their contact to rate the firm's performance on key aspects of the proposal according to a numerical scale, or a rating such as 'strong', 'average' and 'weak'. Others decide simply to ask open-ended questions. Both methods are unsatisfactory.

A questionnaire is too impersonal, inflexible and imprecise to provide the detailed feedback you need. It's also hard work for the prospective client, even if the questionnaire is multiple choice; after a lengthy tender process, the last thing your contact will feel like doing is answering a lengthy set of questions – particularly for a losing firm. You may think that it's the least the organisation can do for you after all the effort you have put in, but all the same it is better to avoid trying their patience.

The reasons why clients pick one firm over another are varied and complex. Asking them to summarise them on a piece of paper therefore invites an incomplete or even disingenuous response. Are they likely, for instance, to write down in black and white that your firm lost because they thought your manner was arrogant? Will they feel inclined to spell out the fact that you inspired little confidence as the best person to lead the assignment?

Conducting your own debriefing

A second option is to perform the debriefing yourself, either over the telephone or face-to-face. This is probably the most common approach: the team leader will 'phone his contact in the target organisation, thank him for his time and help during the tender, and ask to discuss the reasons why the firm lost.

This is a usually an embarrassing experience for both parties, and tends to make for short and inconclusive debriefings. You probably do not wish to explore the subject in any depth and may find it difficult to keep your injured pride in check. And the interviewee is unlikely to give full or frank answers to your questions.

If it was you who were the problem, the contact is hardly likely to admit it. He may therefore duck the issue, or attempt to pin the blame on another member of the team. Alternatively, he may resort to unhelpful cliches, such as 'We didn't feel the chemistry was right', or fabricate some other anodyne explanation rather than tell you the truth.

The argument against conducting your own debriefing is

straightforward: you are unlikely to ask the most difficult questions; and even if you do, the interviewee is unlikely to answer them.

Sending a colleague

Asking a colleague to conduct the debriefing is a little more satisfactory. If the team was the sticking point, the interviewee can at least say so without risking personal offence to the person asking the questions.

Nevertheless, the discussion is still likely to be quite emotionally charged. Your colleague will probably feel as depressed as you do that the firm has lost, while the decision-makers may be reluctant to make any major criticisms of your firm's approach to one of its senior representatives. It is also possible that team members will feel defensive about a colleague investigating their performance in this way. Sending a colleague is better than nothing, but it is not ideal.

Using a third party

The most effective way to overcome these obstacles is to assign the interviewing task to an independent third party, such as a consultant.

While your contact is more likely to be open with someone who is independent of your firm, this is not to say that he will be prepared to divulge all the details of the process, or to be totally honest about how the final decision was taken. This is where the skill of the interviewer is critical: fully briefed and preferably familiar with your industry and your competitors, the consultant should be able to read between the lines and make a judgement about whether the interviewee is telling the whole story. In order to draw the right inferences, it is essential that the interview is conducted in person rather than over the telephone.

Experience suggests that most organisations are happy to take part in debriefing exercises. The relevant individual will usually be quite flattered that the firm is prepared to go to these lengths in order to seek his views, and there is a growing understanding among organisations regularly putting work out to tender that they are under a moral obligation to make time for activities of this sort. The process will also usually reflect well on the firm itself, since it will reinforce the impression that your approach is thorough and professional, and that you take proposals seriously.

What do we need to find out?

Fig. 10.1 lists some of the key issues which debriefings should cover. The substance of the questions and the way they are

---

1 **What were your reasons for going out to tender?**

2 **Which firms did you invite to tender and why?**

3 **Who was involved within your organisation in decision-making, and what was the method of appraisal (formal 'scoring', a qualitative approach etc)?**

4 **What were your reasons for structuring the proposal process in the way that you did (e.g. site visits/document/oral presentation)?**

5 **What impressions did you gain of the firm during its site visits, and how did it compare with the other contenders?**

6 **What did you think of the firm's written submission – and those of the other firms?**

7 **What were the criteria used for deciding which firms would be asked to make an oral presentation?**

8 **To what extent did each firm's performance in the presentation either reinforce or contradict earlier impressions?**

9 **Which factors governed the final selection?**

10 **What could the losing firms have done to have improved their performance?**

Figure 10.1   Key debriefing questions

expressed will need to be tailored to the circumstances, but aim to get a response to each of the ten questions listed.

The list is not definitive, but should prove helpful in providing a structure for the discussion. In practice, interviewees tend to concentrate on particular aspects of the process – the interviewer should allow them to elaborate on these in detail, as they may shed light on other areas.

For example, questions about your firm's performance at the presentation should provide some useful insights into how the key members of your team came across as individuals. Did they convey a sense of purpose and authority; were they in command of their facts? Did they strike the decision-makers as people whom they would be happy to work with, or inspire only limited confidence? As with site visits, the discussion should be structured in a way which permits more significant issues to be explored at the expense of those which are only of subsidiary importance.

Make sure that the interviewer also asks about other opportunities to work together. That will help you to decide whether the organisation should still be treated as a new business target.

LEARNING FROM THE EXPERIENCE

The debriefing over, you need to ensure that the key messages are fully disseminated and understood. Distribute the debriefing notes around the firm, together with a memorandum setting out your own observations and conclusions.

Get the proposal team together one last time and compare what the debriefing says about your performance with your own assessment. Try not to sanitise the feedback or gloss over your mistakes; make sure everyone knows what was done well and badly, and which factors influenced the outcome.

Again, do not turn the session into a witch-hunt. Where specific individuals clearly made significant errors, be diplomatic and have a word with them privately. Everyone makes mistakes; what matters is that they don't make them a second time.

Where the volume of tender activity justifies it, you might introduce a regular internal bulletin which summarises the findings from recent proposal debriefings. Each debriefing note should be placed in the firm's library and catalogued according to industry sector and/or project type. That way, proposal teams can refer to the material when planning their approach to future tenders.

However successful or experienced your firm has become in competitive tendering, there are always aspects which could have been handled better and new messages to take into account. Make sure that the whole firm benefits from your experience.

KEY POINTS

- Stay in contact with the organisation between the oral presentation and the announcement of the result.

- Look for indications that key messages may need to be clarified or supplementary information provided; detailed or repeated questioning during the oral presentation will usually forewarn you of any misunderstandings.

- When asked for more information, make sure it is provided promptly – preferably on the spot or later in the same day.

- If the decision-makers are having difficulty with their final selection, offer to attend a second meeting, make another presentation or perform a mini-project.

- Be alert to additional opportunities suggested by the proposal and debriefing process: don't cut off your links with the organisation because you may have lost.

- After the result is announced, make sure that you debrief both your own team and the organisation, irrespective of whether you have won or lost.

- Bear in mind that more than one individual may need to be debriefed within the target organisation but, in seeking their views, be careful not to be perceived as wasting management time.

- Try to have the debriefing conducted by a third party unconnected with either your firm or the target organisation; this will encourage a candid response.

- Write down the detailed findings from your debriefing and summarise the main points.

- Ensure that your findings are disseminated as widely as possible within your firm, and that they are made readily accessible to others for use in future proposal situations.

- Remember that winning does not imply perfection; every proposal could be improved.

11

PROPOSALS: BUILDING COMPETITIVE ADVANTAGE

SUSTAINING SUCCESS

As we said at the beginning, there is no formula solution to winning proposals. You can considerably increase your chances of success by applying the right principles but, in the final analysis, the competitive edge which in general will win the assignment can be created only through the hard work and thinking that the proposal team devotes to the task.

Of course, there will always be some people who are better at proposing than others. But beware the 'cult of the individual'. We have made the point that there are seldom enough good proposers to go around and potential clients are usually suspicious of those they perceive to be figureheads or proposal specialists. Leaving proposals to an elite minority is therefore no solution. Not only will it make the firm dangerously dependent on a small number of individuals, but it will prevent the replication of skills needed to build competitive advantage in the longer term; and those who are not seen, or don't see themselves, as proposal 'stars' will feel intimidated and alienated. Even if offered the choice, they will prefer not to take part.

A more 'corporate' and unemotive approach is needed. In this connection, there are three initiatives you might consider.

The first is to create a means by which you can measure your success rate over a period of time. Make an assessment of your performance to date: go back through past proposals, endeavour to quantify the proportion you won in terms of both volume and value; and establish as far as you can the reasons for success or failure in each case. This will give you a benchmark against which to assess future performance. You may also decide to set a target for, say, the next 12 months. The approach will help to focus attention on overall performance and may to some extent check the invidious tendency for proposers to be judged by their peers only on the outcome of the largest and highest profile tenders.

It is quite possible to lose a well-conceived and conducted proposal and, conversely, to win a poorly-developed one. For this and all the other reasons outlined in the previous chapter, for future proposals establish a system of debriefing which will enable you to develop a precise understanding of the reasons for your wins and losses.

Above all, think about providing support to your people in order to help them improve their proposal techniques. As a minimum, this should involve the dissemination of proposal debriefs and regular reports on the firm's performance as a whole; you might also consider guidance notes, departmental seminars, teach-ins by more experienced proposal practitioners, and sending staff on external courses in writing and presentation skills. Whatever form your programme takes, make sure you include both junior as well as senior professionals – everyone with direct client contact should be involved, and obviously it is important to build for the future.

The growing prevalence of competitive tendering suggests that only those firms prepared to implement root-and-branch initiatives of this sort will succeed in the long term.

WINNING FACTORS

What is it that makes the difference between success and failure?

It has been suggested that competitive tendering is like a cross between courting and sitting an exam; certainly, proposals usually evoke the same piquant mixture of fear and anticipation you might expect to encounter while engaged in these two activities.

However, the former is the better analogy. A competitive tender is actually nothing like an exam, even though it might feel like it. In proposals, it is never enough to reach the passmark – you have to come first. And in order to come first, you have to do more than comply with a set of requirements.

So it often pays for proposers to be as bold in their approach as possible; if you are not prepared to take some risks, resign yourself to coming second on a regular basis. There are few rewards for the conformist or those without the courage to back their convictions.

Of course, a high-risk strategy will only pay dividends if you are sure of your ground and can make a cogent, logical case. To achieve that, you must be prepared to observe, listen and learn, and be sensitive and flexible as well as resolute and single-minded. Above all, put yourself in the potential client's shoes from the very beginning; remember that those responsible for initiating and managing the proposal may be feeling more under pressure than you are. After all, there could be damaging commercial and personal ramifications from their point of view if the tender does not achieve its objectives.

None of this can guarantee that you will win a particular proposal. But, over time, it will ensure that you win many more than your fair share.

INDEX